Ensign Bell in the Peninsular War

Ensign Bell in the Peninsular War

The Experiences of a Young British Soldier of the 34th Regiment 'The Cumberland Gentlemen' in the Napoleonic Wars

George Bell

Ensign Bell in the Peninsular War': The Experiences of a Young British Soldier of the 34th Regiment 'The Cumberland Gentlemen' in the Napoleonic Wars

First Edition

Published by Leonaur Ltd

Material original to this edition and its origination in this form copyright © 2006 Leonaur Ltd

ISBN (10 digit): 1-84677-081-5 (hardcover)
ISBN (13 digit): 978-1-84677-081-4 (hardcover)

ISBN (10 digit): 1-84677-067-X (softcover)
ISBN (13 digit): 978-1-84677-067-8 (softcover)

http://www.leonaur.com

Publishers Notes

In the interests of authenticity, the spellings, grammar and place names used in this book have been retained from the original edition.

The opinions of the author represent a view of events in which he was a participant related from his own perspective; as such the text is relevant as an historical document.

The views expressed in this book are not necessarily those of the publisher.

Contents

I Join the 'Cumberland Gentlemen'	7
To the Peninsula	12
The March Begins	18
We Meet the French	24
'Ciudad Rodrigo Must Be Stormed'	28
Bone Soup	37
Towards Badajos	39
The Assault on Badajos	43
The Sacking of Badajos	48
Chasing the French	52
Truxillo	58
Campaigns With Quill	61
Dining with Madmen	69
Salamanca	72
Routed Out of Yepes	79
To Madrid	85
Retreat!	88
Farewell Portugal	105
The Battle of Vittoria	110
Pursuit	115
Spoils	121
To the Pyrenees	124
Fighting in the Mountains	132
Pampeluna	139
War in the Passes	143
Nivelle	150
We Enter France	168
Saint Pierre	173
After the Nive	179
Orthes	185
Aire	189
Marching Through France	200
The Battle of Toulouse	204
Napoleon Abdicates	212
The End of the Campaign	220

Chapter One
I Join the 'Cumberland Gentlemen'

The London Gazette of the 11th March 1811 proclaimed 'George Bell, gentleman, to be Ensign in the 34th Regiment of Foot, by command of His Majesty King George the Third'. On the 11th of March I was at a public school, when some one came and gave me the above information.

So soon as I collected my senses, I jumped up, broke my way into the presence of the great *Dominie*, bid him a hasty farewell, shook hands with my class companions, and bolted out of the house, no one seeming to know what it was all about until I was clear away, and sent back a newspaper with the Gazette, which fully explained my hasty retreat from thraldom.

Six days after the 11th of March I was just seventeen years of age, an independent military gentleman, let loose upon the world with the liberal pay of 5s. 3d. a day, less income-tax, which has never been increased from that day to this.

I had an official letter very soon to join my regimental depot without delay, signed Harry Calvert, Adjutant-General.

So I went off that night by the mail a hundred miles' journey, to bid them farewell at the beautiful paternal residence on the banks of Lough Erin. Here I only remained two days: there was weeping and lamentation over-much at my departure; but it was the tender custom in Ireland long ago. The family circle saw me off, at the end of the long avenue, all pretty cheery until we heard the mail-coach horn in the distance, when the ladies began a fresh lamentation, which set me going until I nearly cried my eyes out.

I was now fairly off, and with my pocket full of money, so I began to brighten up by the time the coach stopped for the night, for this hundred-mile journey occupied two days.

This Royal Mail-coach was horsed with a pair of old Irish hunters, carried four passengers inside, and two guards in Royal livery behind, with a box of blunderbuss firearms and pistols, to protect themselves and the mail-bags; the roads in those days being swarmed by highwaymen. We had no adventure.

After being well furnished with a good kit, and supplied liberally with everything I required, I sailed in the mail-packet for Liverpool, which I reached the third day, after a stormy voyage. It was then the custom for each passenger to carry his own prog; my hamper never was opened, I was so desperately sea-sick, consequently the steward came in for nearly all the good things, and might have set up a cookshop for many a day afterwards.

Safely on English ground for the first time, I enjoyed myself for a couple of days, and then took coach with four spanking horses for Beverley, in Yorkshire, where I joined my depot, and went to drill under the command of an old Sergeant, who used to say that he was preparing me for a great General some day, if I didn't fall on the bed of honour before my time.

I now mounted my uniform for the first time, and when full dressed was ashamed to appear in the streets. I fancied all the people would be laughing at the raw Ensign, with his cocked hat and feather, jack boots, white breeches, sword, and belt; then the sword was always getting between my legs, trying to trip me up as I cautiously went along, not daring to look at any one. I thought myself the observed of all observers, being just bran-new out of the tailor's shop. We were encumbered with many sorts of regimental useless dresses, such as long black cloth leggings, with about two dozens of bright buttons up the outside of each leg! Then, for the evening, tight-fitting white kerseymere pantaloons, and Hessian boots with black silk tassels in front; and, when on duty, a gorget hanging under one's chin.

I was a right jolly fellow when I got all this toggery off my back, and enjoyed myself to the full. We had no mess, lived in lodgings, no restraint on us young fellows, and had, with the 5s. 3d. a day, 6s. a week lodging money, to provide ourselves with respectable quarters.

I found the pretty town of Beverley a most agreeable residence, and never dreamt of leaving it, until one fine morning we heard of the battle of Albuera, in which my regiment was engaged and suffered severely: the gaps of death must be filled; I was one of the number ordered out to fill this vacancy.

The route came upon us all of a heap, in the midst of fun and frolic, to march for Portsmouth, and embark for Portugal. It was twenty-two days' march; and away we went, thoughtless jolly dogs, living at hotels on the road, which astonished the 5s. 3d. a day! The marches were long at times, and many a day I almost dropped footsore and weary, which I never confessed. We always had breakfast at the half-way house, ordered by one of our men sent in advance; halted and formed up in military order before we marched into the town or village, swords drawn, and our drum and fife playing martial music. We had all the little boys and girls half a mile round pressing into the ranks to hear the band, as they said, and see the soldiers. After one hour's halt, and 2s worth of first-rate morning meal, leaving the jolly landlord very little profit, we continued our march, the same orderly going on to announce our approach at the billeting town, and to order dinner for the army! The march from Brigg to Lincoln I shall never forget-twenty-four miles of a straight line, the steeple that held Big Tom always in front—only one other march in all my campaigns knocked the life so much out of my feet, and that was a forced night march to Madrid, which I may record hereafter.

The landlords of the hotels always waited personally on us, to know our pleasure about the dinner hour, and what wines we liked best, etc. For my part, I would have been perfectly satisfied with a beef-steak and a pint of ale, but dared not express anything so *infra dig* with a red coat on my back; so left it all to my superiors, and paid my share of the bill with the best grace I could, not being a wine drinker, and finding the 5s. 3d. only about equal to satisfy the servants and some minor things by the way. At Oxford we were met by another detachment of different regiments on the same route, going to the wars; here we amalgamated and had a great jollification dinner-party. I could only consent to any proposal, having no voice of my own in the matter, paid three times the amount of the usual bill, and had a crashing headache next morning to cheer me. I was astonished to see what some of those fellows could drink, and not seem to feel the worse; one lad of my own age and standing got screwed every night—but he did not last long! I gave him many a lecture, being his senior officer by one week, but could not make any impression on a lad that sucked the money, *i.e.* going to bed with a bottle of brandy.

We had charming weather all the way—old women came toddling out by the wayside as we passed, crying out—"There goes a few more lambs to the slaughter, poor things!" which only caused some merriment amongst the soldiers, who were the most thoughtless set of dogs I ever saw since or before—not one of them ever returned to England!

We finished our march at Portsmouth, and were billeted at an hotel called the *'Blue Posts'*. I was very tired and very green in those days; I went to bed early, left my door unlocked, threw my clothes on a chair, and was soon in my dreams. I had £25 with me—all I was worth in the world; my pocket-book contained this treasure—it had many folds, in which my money was divided. When I turned out in the morning, I was nervously horrified at seeing my clothes scattered about the floor. I approached the examination with dread and saw at once the shadow of, to me, a great calamity. Some very unkind but thoughtful person had entered my bedroom while asleep, to count my money and square my accounts, extracted a ten pound Bank of England note, for the trouble and risk, and left, but perhaps overlooked, the balance of £15 which lay in another part of the book, so that I was, not altogether bankrupt. I had a very good guess who this wretched robber was, and might have put my hand upon him, but I had no proof. I made my report to the commanding officer of our party; but he seemed to doubt my tale; nor would he make any inquiry, which nettled me more severely than the loss I sustained.

Chapter Two
To the Peninsula

A week in Portsmouth reduced my £15. I had £7 10s. to pay for my share of sea-stock; the balance I changed into dollars, and embarked, in light marching order, on board the *Arethusa*, a rotten old transport of 300 tons. We had a gale of wind, of course, in the Bay of Biscay-O, and put back to Falmouth for some little repairs and more prog. We all subscribed and laid in a few sacks of potatoes, flour, and fresh meat. I took a Sunday walk in the country, strolled into a farm-house, while the jolly fat landlord and his dame were at their roast beef dinner and ale; they looked a little surprised at seeing a young fellow in a red coat at the door in that part of the country, but asked me to come in and taste their roast beef. I was always hungry in those days, and took my seat at the little round table, in the neat, clean, well-furnished kitchen; there was an air of comfort about it one hardly ever sees in any other country; they asked me a great many questions, every one then being interested in the war. I told them all I knew; and when I was going, they both shook my hands with some interest. I gave them thanks, bid them good-bye, left half-a-crown on the table, and went back to my den upon the waters.

Our commanding officer had a cabin about the size of a coffin to himself; thirteen of us commissioned officers of different corps messed and slept in the cuddy, a sort of dog-kennel, where we washed by turns in the morning. One very lazy fellow, a Lieutenant of the 39th Regiment, who swung in a cot over the table, never could be got up in time to have the saloon swept and garnished for breakfast. I told him that the next time I was on duty as the orderly officer, if he was not up at the first bugle sound I would cut him down. The weather now was very warm, and this Paddy from Cork slept without any shirt, whether from long habit or economy I did not inquire. However, as usual, he could not be roused up, so I cut the head-rope of his cot, and down he came whop on the table; he was furious, grasped a knife and chased me up on deck. I ran into the rigging like a cat. He flourished his knife, the people stared and thought him deranged. I explained in four or five words: 'I cut down Mr. Lazybones.' Then there was a general yell of laughter; he dived below. I had only obeyed orders, so he dared not dispute the matter, and was never late again.

The voyage was a long one, owing to a convoy of all sorts of small craft going to Lisbon.

'What have you on board?' said our skipper to a wretched-looking tub from Cork.

'Fruit and timber,' says Pat.

'What sort are they?'

'Birch brooms and praties, admiral,' speaking through an old tin pot with the bottom knocked out of it, and then a roar of a laugh on the potato barge. We were on short commons before we made the land, and our potatoes were counted out every day until we entered the Tagus. A joyful day it was to get out of prison. Ten miles up the river, and we anchored off the Block Horse Square. The scenery all around the country is beautiful—very beautiful. The city stands on the north bank of the Tagus, here nine miles wide, and could shelter ten thousand ships. No end to the multitude of churches, chapels, convents, and monasteries. What a good people these ought to be, with so many friars, priests, and nuns scattered amongst them to look after their morals!

We landed under a broiling sun. The men were sent into an old monastery, and bivouacked in the corridors.

The officers got billets in different parts of the city; mine was in a very ugly quarter town, and had a cut-throat-like entrance, through a long dark vaulted passage. I made my way up a long flight of dark stairs, knocked at an iron portal very like a prison, presented my billet, which was examined by a Portuguese nigger, with a grin. The door closed until 'Massa see ticket', when, after some delay, I was admitted, and shown into a small room with a wee sleeping-cot in the corner, and there left in solitude.

Not knowing three words of the Portuguese lingo, and no one coming to pay me a visit or give me a welcome, I went out for a ramble, lost my way, and wandered about until ten o'clock at night, when I most fortunately met an officer going to our ship, who took me on board for the night.

Next day I found my quarters, took the bearings, and went in search of my party, but could not find one of them. The weather was broiling hot, the market full of the choicest fruits—oranges, grapes, melons, peaches, greengage, an abundant supply of all sorts, enough for an army. Like a very imprudent young spoon, I went right at them all, and feasted too freely; then made my way out of the town into the country, about half a league, to enjoy the breeze. Seeing a fine vineyard, and the gate open, I went in without ceremony. The senor was there, recumbent in a beautiful arbour, while his people were busy making wine. He very politely asked me to be seated, talked a great deal, I suppose about the army of England. All I understood were a few words, as Wellington, and the *guerre*, and Marshall Soult. I felt myself very small, not being able to speak to this gentleman; but there was no remedy, so I resolved at once to learn the language, and thus quieted my mind.

He ordered one of his men to present me a goblet of wine, which I drank off to his health. He returned the compliment, only tasting his cup, and we parted, my host accompanying me to the gate, hat in hand. I found my home, went to roost early, was taken seriously ill in the night, and lay there for many days. No one of my party knew where I was; I could not speak, and the only person I saw was a little black maid, who brought me some rice-water daily, and put it down by my bedside. The fruit and the wine nearly finished me. Had I been in the hands of a doctor, he would most likely have put me under the sod—particularly a medico of this country, who are celebrated for their ignorance in the profession. Ditto in Spain, where they continue the old Sangrado system, phlebotomize nearly to death, shut you up tight in a dark room without breath of fresh air, and give you plenty of hot water to drink. The patient dies, of course!

When I was able to crawl, I went out in search of the monastery, met one of my men, who conducted me to it, and there found all my people. Some thought I was kidnapped, others that I had deserted, and many were the surmises what had become of G.B. The old captain, our commanding officer, never troubled himself about me. I found out for the first time now, that we were all entitled to rations, and the Captain B-- had been drawing mine and making use of them like an honest fellow. He was our Paterfamilias, an old soldier who had been at home on sick leave, and knew the country and its ways and means, up to every dodge, and how to take precious good care of himself. He told us many stories about his former campaigns, and how he leathered the French. Subsequently we were informed it was but his playful way of amusing 'Johnny Newcomes', as he had never yet had the good fortune of slaying a *Mounseer* in battle. He had the soubriquet in the regiment of 'Bloody Mick, who killed all the French with his great big stick'.

I went back to my billet with my servant to take away my few traps, and settle down in the old monastery with my companions. I was met by the *padrone*, who inquired after my health, and asked me to dinner at two o'clock with his family. This was done by the aid of a Portuguese and English dictionary. I made my appearance, and got Benjamin's portion, the first course—that was, a plate-load of rice and oil, chopped onion and garlic, too savoury for an invalid. I put it gently aside, which rather astonished the landlady, who was evidently taken aback that I did not relish this part of her dinner. However, there was something else without that most delicious flavour of Portuguese garlic—good bread and palatable wine and fruit; and so I finished my first and last meal in the house of a Portuguese gentleman.

I gladly embraced the opportunity of housing myself now in the monastery amongst the monks and friars—a lazy, indolent crew, with their bull-necks, bare shaven crown's, sandals, cowls, and white rope girdles and rosary. They lived in their cells, or very comfortable little rooms, while we occupied the corridors and galleries. I slept on the flags with my martial cloak around me! It was all the bed and bedding I had; the climate was blazing hot, and the broad flags kept me cool.

We had a camp-kettle in which we cooked all our rations together; there was an abundance of the finest vegetables, very cheap, so that, with some rice in addition, we turned out excellent soup and *bouilli*. Each of us had a tin dish, an iron spoon, knife and fork, without any other incumbrance of this kind. Sometimes we got a bullock's head to add to the rations, which when cold also gave us a breakfast.

I joined another lad in the purchase of a *boura* to carry our baggage, i.e. in English, a donkey. My camp equipage was small when the broadside of a donkey carried it all. This purchase cleared me out. I had not a dollar left, and had no opportunity of seeing any of the sights, or enjoying any of the pleasures of a Lisbon life. I became a sort of a monk myself, visiting those old crows every day. They supposed me a good Roman Catholic, because I spoke a little Latin to them, and confessed myself an Irishman.

One question they never forgot to ask, 'Are you an Irishman?' They consider all Irishmen Roman Catholics; regarding myself, they were quite out of their reckoning, for there never was a more staunch, loyal Protestant subject of the Queen of England than G.B.

Chapter Three
The March Begins

The route came for us at last, and all the convalescent men from Belem depot joined us for the march, and away we went in the middle of the night, to get it over before the burning early sun of the morrow. It was weary work ploughing through the deep sands all the way. How I looked back to home, sweet home! and to the noble horses I used to ride there at pleasure. Any money now for 'Billy Button', the orderly pony, always ready saddled in the stable for general use.

The marches were sometimes very long and dreary, and provoking. No one knew the distance; meeting a solitary peasant now and then we would ask, '*Quantas leaguas, senor, a Sacavem?*'

Answer, '*Dos leaguas e pokito, senor*' (two leagues and a bit); march on another league and meet *pizano* the second, and ask the same question, '*O senor, Sacavem, tres leaguas e no mas*' (just three leagues)!

No milestones, no hotels, inns, or refreshment houses; we knew, however, that there was a town in the distance somewhere, and that we must reach it. Our Captain, commanding officer, was well mounted and always had some grog, etc., in his haversack, which he seemed to enjoy at the usual halting-place half-way, under a shady tree, all alone! Sergeant Bolland, a fine old soldier of our regiment, returning from Lisbon, aided us in many ways, gave us good advice in the arrangement of our future campaign and as to how to take care of ourselves, for as he said, 'this is all pleasure to what is before us, if I may judge of the past'—he had been wounded at Albuera.

We went merrily on for many days, living on our rations, until we arrived at Portalegre, the headquarters of the 34th, and such a nice handy well-disciplined corps, with high-caste officers, all well seasoned and experienced in the late campaigns.

I had letters of introduction to Colonel Fenwick and other officers of note and standing, all of whom received me cordially, and I was no longer a stranger. The Colonel asked me to breakfast on arrival, when I gave him my history from the starting-point, and a sample of such an appetite that must have astonished him, and I feared would prevent him from showing me any more such attentions; but he was always kind—an amiable man, a good and gallant soldier, decided in character, just and impartial.

I was appointed to the company of 'Moyle Sherer', then a Lieutenant, a gentleman, a scholar, an author, and a most zealous soldier.

I now settled down in my billet, commenced my orderly duties, and endeavoured to make myself comfortable and to prepare for the storm of war, then sweeping over unhappy Spain. I had nothing to trouble me but a big appetite, for which my ration was quite insufficient; three-quarters of a pound of lean beef, half bone at times, a pound of brown bread or biscuit, and half a gill of rum; I often finished the whole dish at a sitting, and got up from the noble repast very hungry. The beef or the bread never was weighed; a certain quantity was served out to each company; say the company was fifty strong, the meat was cut into fifty pieces, and spread on the turf. One man turned his back on the rations not to see them, another called out;

'This—say Tom Johns,' and Tom picked up his morsel of beef; 'This—Jack Simmons,' and there was a great roar of a laugh, for it was nearly all a marrow bone! 'This—Mr. G.B.,' and so on, all fair play between officers and men.

I had a chair and a table, and a sort of a bed in my little room on which I slept soundly—dogs always go to sleep when hungry!

I had no books and was very idle; it was not customary in those days in the army to read the Bible; I don't think that I saw one for three years, so that Portugal or Spain had no fault to find with us on this score! However, there were some good and pious men to be found, who were not ashamed to

Kneel, remote, upon the simple sod,
And sue, in forma pauperis, to God.

We Subs were a sociable class of bipeds; we had dinner parties, and evening parties, and dancing parties, and horse-racing parties all very simple in their way, and not attended with any expense; for instance, 'Come to dinner tomorrow in camp fashion', that means, send your rations, your servant, chair, knife, fork, spoon and plate (not plates); three or four rations of beef made better soup than three-quarters of a pound with a bone in it; then there might be a bit of liver and bacon, and some roast tatties, and roars of laughter and fun; so much for subaltern dinner in service fifty years ago.

Those who could afford an evening party had brandy and cigars, or wine and crackers for their guests, plenty of chat about the past, the present, and the future; and some comic songs.

The bottles being all drained, the evening closed, and good night was said: some one of the guests adding, 'You will all come to me tomorrow night.'

The girls were very fond of dancing: we sometimes all joined for a ball, and invited young ladies and their mammas to look after them. We had no band; a flute and guitar filled the orchestra; there was some lemonade and cakes—to refresh the *senoritas*—all they wished for; all they expected. The priests were always reluctant and jealous to see any of their fair flock mixing with heretics; the ladies quite differed in opinion!

The Derby never created more fear or excitement than our race-ground on the olive plain. All the *Tats* in the garrison went to the post very smart, and ready to win the bag of dollars hanging on the big olive-tree; first away often last in the race—the real winner sometimes losing his race by dismounting before coming to the scale to be weighed—one or two disappearing as bolters amongst the trees. A jockey with perhaps a red night-cap going right off to his stable in the town, and knocking down two priests in the gateway. Then the donkey race; every Jock sitting with his face to the tail, a smart fellow running in front with a bunch of carrots, and so we passed our time.

I had a letter from home now, and no little sympathy expressed for my loss at Portsmouth. I might draw for my allowance in advance; it was enough for me—more than I deserved; but far away less than the young gentlemen of the present day in the army receive, or demand, or cannot do without! I never went into debt in all my life—I knew that it was dangerous; and, not being able to pay, dishonourable. I had recourse to my old commanding officer, Captain B--, for some money—he was the only one who seemed to understand those pecuniary affairs with advantage. He charged me 6s. sterling for every dollar he gave me, a dollar being worth 4s. 2d.! I was now rich for the present, and fared well, and had an evening party—no very great enjoyment to me, for I detest brandy and cigars.

I made myself happy in a way until October, when there was a flare-up with the French.

General Girard made too free with our side of the country, and began to poach on our guard. The 2nd Division, commanded by Lieutenant-General Sir Rowland Hill, was let loose to hunt him out of our district. The rainy season had commenced, and the weather was dreadful. We marched all the day, and lay down on the wet sod by night, which rather surprised and alarmed me, expecting to be under cover in some civilised way after our day's work, instead of herding with the beasts of the field. I had an old boat cloak and a blanket for my bed and bedding. I never had more, but sometimes less, for the next three years.

'We have made a raw and rainy beginning of our campaign,' said Richardson, my chum; 'how did you sleep?'

'Slept like a fish,' I said; 'I believe they sleep best in water.'

'Bravo!' said he; 'you'll do.'

I thought in my own mind I might do for a night or two more, but I would soon be done in a bivouac in such weather; however, I kept that secret to myself.

David Richardson was an old soldier, and had passed through a campaign. 'Come over to my quarters,' he said, 'and have a cup of tea; it will take the chill out of your old bones; you look blue in the face.'

Near at hand his kettle was boiling under an olive-tree, and a pork chop in the frying-pan—very savoury. 'Shake a little pepper on it, Ned, and be quick; the bugle will sound directly, and get the other plate.'

'There's only one, sir,' replied Ned; 'You know we left in light marching order.'

'You have the advantage of me, Davey,' added I, 'having seen service, and knowing how to forage. As for me, I am indeed in light marching condition, and have nothing but my haversack, containing my three days' rations cooked —but where in the world did you fall in with this savoury meat?'

'Well,' he said, 'my man Ned there has a sharp eye and a sharp bayonet, and if those pigs will intrude upon us at night, it is at their own risk; you will learn more about these little private affairs time enough.' Bugle sounds. 'There, Ned, get your breakfast quickly, and throw that leg of pork into the bag, and load the donkey.'

Chapter Four
We Meet the French

We continued our march in this way for a week. Our ration of rum at night kept the life in us. There were no tents in the army in those days; it was all bivouac, pleasant enough in hot weather and dry ground; but this was an exceptional case, and not meant to continue. The rain kept along with us. I was never thoroughly dry, yet there is nothing that keeps out wet like a blanket; there was no such thing as an india-rubber or a macintosh A.D. 1811, and as for anything else called waterproof, it was all fudge. We never undressed of course, but just pushed on, apparently having the right scent, as the men would constantly say, 'I smell those crappos, they can't be far off.' They had been keeping one day ahead of us, and left behind them a perfume of tobacco, onions, etc., that could not be mistaken.

On the evening of the 27th of October we got close to their heels; it rained all the day, and in the dusk we halted on ploughed ground. 'Pile arms; keep perfectly quiet; light no fires; no drum to beat; no bugle to sound', were the orders passed through the ranks. I was very tired; threw myself up against the side of a bank ditch, dived into my haversack, where I had in reserve a piece of cold bullock's liver and salt, some biscuit, and a very small allowance of rum, so I was not so badly off.

All was still, and cold, and cheerless, until about two o'clock in the morning of the 28th, when the word was gently passed through all regiments: 'Stand to your arms!' The whole division was now in silent motion, and moved on to the plain some few miles, pretty close to the enemy, who were quartered and encamped in and about the little town of 'Arroyo-Molino'. The division was now divided into three brigades, cavalry on flanks and centre. It was just the dawn of day, with a drizzling rain. We could just see our men to call the roll.

Our gallant and worthy General, riding along our front, said, 'Are you all ready?'

'Yes, sir.'

'Uncase your colours, and prime the load.'

All this looked very serious, and I began to have a queer feeling of mortal danger stirring my nerves. As I took the king's colour in charge, being senior ensign, the Major said, 'Now my lads, hold those standards fast, and let them fly out when you see the enemy.'

Away we went across the plain to be baptised in blood. Our skirmishers in advance had come upon the French outlying pickets, and had begun operations. A cannon-shot came rattling past, making a hissing noise, such as I had never heard before. Four sergeants supported the colours in battle; my old friend Bolland from Beverley was one of them.

I said, 'What's that, Bolland?'

'Only the morning gun, sir; they're just coming on them now.'

A little onwards, and I saw two men cut across by that last shot, the first I had ever seen killed. I was horrified, but said nothing.

The French were getting ready to be off again when our advance got up to their pickets and began the quarrel. Their horses were saddled and tied to the olive-trees, infantry gathering from different points for their alarm-post—artillery taking up position—all getting on the defensive, when they were skilfully hemmed in on three sides; behind the little town the 71st and 92nd Regiments brought up their left shoulders, and came pouring into the streets with a destructive fire; the French were now falling by fifties, but fighting and struggling hard to maintain their ground.

We had lined the garden walls, and kept pitching into their ranks while our cavalry cut off their retreat; they formed squares, but our artillery mashed them up and the cavalry gave them no time to re-form; a thick mist rolled down the craggy steep mountain behind the town; there was a terrifying cheer, such as is not known except amongst British troops on the battleground; it drowned the clatter of musketry, while the driving storm carried with it the enemy up this *sierra*, the 28th and 34th Regiments at their heels.

We pressed them so closely that they threw off their knapsacks, turned round, and fired into us; still our men pushed on until this body of Girard's brave army dropped their firelocks, dispersed, and as many as could got clear away over the mountains. Below, the 50th and 39th Regiments were tormenting the unfortunate French with the bayonet and making prisoners; the 13th Dragoons captured their artillery as they made a dash for escape, which was simply done by shooting a mule in each gun; the 9th Dragoons and German hussars charged and dispersed their cavalry with great loss, taking many prisoners; Prince D'Aremberg, making his escape in a light carriage, was followed by a few of our dragoons; one of them rode up to the door and desired him in English to halt; the reply was a bullet through his head-a useless and rather cowardly endeavour to save his liberty, for instantly one of his mules was shot, which brought him to a single anchor, as the sailors say. He was then handed out of his coach, not by a powdered footman, but at the point of an English broadsword, and his comfortable nest immediately plundered, the soldiers being exasperated for the untimely death of a comrade while doing his duty.

Girard was wounded, but fought nobly until he saw that any further resistance was useless; then, having given his men the order to disperse—*Sauve qui peut*—fled and saved himself; 600 men, the remains of 3,000 of the most valiant and chosen troops of France, saved themselves by flight.

Our trophies this misty morning were General Le Bron, the Prince D'Aremberg, 40 officers, 1,500 men, all their artillery, baggage, and commissariat stores. I was very proud of having unfurled the colours of my regiment before the French for the first time, and cheered loudly with the rest when I saw them run! Our loss did not exceed 70 men left *hors de combat*—not many killed.

Chapter Five
'Ciudad Rodrigo Must Be Stormed'

It was a little remarkable that the two regiments—34th English and 34th French—happened to meet face to face in mortal combat. The *Parley Vous*, as our men called them, had no chance against the old Cumberland infantry. We took very many of them prisoners, with all their band and drums and the drum-major and his long cane. They are still, or part of them, in possession of the regiment.

I know of only one officer now alive who was present on that day, and he bought from a soldier a very valuable diamond crescent for three dollars, taken out of the Prince D--'s carriage. There were many valuables for sale at a low figure that day! I had not a dollar left, or would have given it cheerfully for a loaf of bread, little expecting that I would soon have one for nothing. Our Commissary bought plenty of flour at the mill, 'Arroyo-Molino', and set all the bakers to work to give the troops a ration of fresh bread and an extra ration of rum after their morning's amusement. I was drying my wet duds in the village when my eye caught the sight of a cart-load of bread going by, and a Portuguese soldier behind in the act of stealing a loaf. I watched until he performed the successful operation, when I gave such a yell and a rush, he thought me the Provost-Marshal, dropped the loaf, and ran for it. I continued the cry of 'Halt, *Ladrone*', until he was too far gone to see or know what use I made of it!

Lieutenant Strenowitz, an Austrian officer on General Hill's staff, always too dashing, was made prisoner. He was brave and enterprising, useful, and very clever in reconnoitring the enemy at any time. He had been dodging the movements of Girard all along, and was well known, having abandoned the French army in Spain to join the Patidas, and liable by the laws of war to death. Sir Rowland, anxious to save him, frankly applied to General Drouet, who, although smarting under his late disaster, released him. A noble generosity, worthy of being recorded in letters of gold.

The 34th now took charge of all the French prisoners, officers and men. The former accepted parole; the latter we locked up in the church, a goodly congregation for the old padre. Yesterday, perhaps, they were robbing his hen-roost, and today certainly teasing his church-toggery—indeed, before the day was closed, they had arranged a theatrical troop, and were performing a play, all rejoicing in the expectation and hope of being escorted to their future banishment by British troops, being under bodily fear of the Spaniards, who would, as they well knew, have bayoneted every man of them that fell out of the ranks; for they had a long account to settle with these French marauders.

The following day we had a rest, and the prisoners opened a bazaar in the church to dispose of, perhaps, all their unlawful gains. It was a great day for the church and for the priests when those fellows departed; every one of them seemed to have a watch for sale, gold or silver, and a great variety of *bijouterie*. There were some great bargains going, but I had not a dollar to get a single kind remembrance of those dear departing friends! My regiment escorted them down to Portugal. By the way they were very cheery, and went to church every night for safety!

On a pinch we always turned the churches to useful and good account. The commissariat, mules, and stores of biscuit and rum were lodged there for nights, weeks, and months, as required, the padres looking in now and then, crossing themselves right-centre and left, with a wailing sort of grunt, seeing their confession-boxes filled with sacks of barley and kegs of rum, the mules picketed on one side, big cooking-fires on the other, and a pleasant smell of fried pork and garlic! The only priestly sound left in the temple was the bell-ringing, every mule having a dozen or more of them as part of his trappings; and pleasant music it was to us many a starry night on the lonely march to hear the muleteers coming along through the cork woods, singing plaintive strains, accompanied by the light guitar. The muleteer is a fine, honest, independent fellow, well made, quaintly dressed, always gay, strong, and active, and very fond of music and dancing when time admits. But he never neglects his work, carries his guitar, sits between two bags of biscuit, both legs on one side, singing a serenade, and twitching his own heart with something plaintive, or perhaps with a *fandango*, the Castilian Maid, or a *bolero*.

The French officers, being all on parole, conducted themselves with great propriety. They messed with the Colonel, Major, and one or two of the senior officers who had means of adding something to the rations. They were under no restraint, and their old soldiers were very careful in not attempting to straggle or fall out by the way, knowing what a sharp look-out the Spaniards had after their liberty. We delivered them all over in safety to another escort in Portugal, returned to Estremadura, and took up quarters in the old town of Albuquerque, with the 28th Regiment, or 'Slashers'.

Every regiment and division had its cognomen; the 2nd, Lord Hill's Division, was called 'the Surprisers', after the affair of Arroyo de Molino; 3rd, or Buffs, 'the Resurrection Men', so many of them returned to the ranks after Albuera. They had been returned missing, but the truth was having taken a brilliant part in that day's big fight, and finding the French retreating through the woods and forest, they pursued them until night, and many of the old Buffs who lost their way in the dark, bivouacked, and came carelessly back to their old ground the next and following days, sat down upon the sod, and went to work to clean and polish up their old flint firelocks for another day; and then inquired after yesterday's rations; for they were very hungry after hunting 'them frog-eaters through the woods—bad luck to them!' The 50th always went by the name of the 'Dirty Half-hundred'—they had black facings.

The 34th, 'the Cumberland Gentlemen' had certainly some of the most select and high-caste officers I ever met in the army—such brave and zealous men too; such as Colonels Maister and Fenwick, Willett, Wyat, Fancourt, Egerton, Sherer, Baron, Worsley—Jolliff, the most liberal paymaster, and the clever surgeon, Luscombe; Sullivan and Eccles, bravest of the brave; Norton, Day, *cum multis aliis*. I love to record their honoured names, being myself, I believe, the last man of that generation that I know of living, unless it be Captain Norton, the inventor of an exploding shell, about which he hoped to gain a name and some emolument, after many years of incessant toil. Not being in the dress circle, I believe all his labour was in vain, and his talent pooh-poohed.

At Albuquerque we got the English newspapers with an account of our exploit at Arroyo-Molino, and wasn't I proud to see Sir Rowland Hill's despatch in print, with the few words, which never escaped my memory, *viz.* 'where the 28th and 34th Regiments eminently distinguished themselves'?

Albuquerque was a very old town, at one period of some importance. It was walled all round, and had a castle of defence, crumbling away like the old walls. In the castle, which stood high, there was a square tower standing still much higher, commanding a most extensive view of the country on towards Badajos (pronounced by the Spaniards Badahos). On the top of this tower there was always an officer on the look-out from before daylight until ten o'clock, with telescope in hand, to watch any movement of the French coming over the plain, a duty not very agreeable to early risers! On many a cold morning I have got up to take this duty for one of my own brother officers better off and more provident than myself, with the understanding that I was to breakfast with him when relieved; for the truth may be told, I had not myself a breakfast to eat, and really nothing at this time but my one scanty meal *per diem*, and that was my bit of ration beef, which I fried in a pan with water for want of a spoonful of oil. My money was all expended long ago. Our pay was months in arrears. My time was not come to draw for my home allowance, and I would not ask for a penny in advance, although I knew it would have been cheerfully granted.

About this time, Drouet came down to forage the province with 14,000 men, and to throw supplies into Badajos. We left our dry quarters, and sallied forth to meet him, Sir Rowland Hill intending to give him battle. On our way to Merida we fell in with a battalion of French infantry in a fog, who were out foraging. We could see nothing. They felt our advance guard as we came up, and left some few wounded prisoners, who told the tale. As the fog rose, we saw them retiring over the plain in the greatest order. Having a good start of us, our cavalry were called to the front, and slipped at them; the French retiring double quick in quarter-distance column. On the near approach of the 14th Light Dragoons, they formed square, and waited the charge, which was repulsed by a volley, leaving some empty saddles. While the cavalry were reforming for another charge, the French again formed quarter-distance column, and went off at the double. The 14th went at them again on two sides; for they whipped into square in a moment, but as unsuccessfully as at first. This play was repeated three times without any success, when our guns came up from the rear, unlimbered, and sent a few round shot into their ranks, which left them short forty men; but the rest got clear away into Merida. I don't remember our loss; but I saw many of our men and horses killed and wounded as we passed by Nevoux, which was the name of the brave French colonel who commanded, was decorated with the Legion of Honour for his gallant conduct on this occasion.

Honourable retreats in war, they say, are in no ways inferior to brave charges, as having less of fortune, more of discipline, and as much of valour.

We marched on and took possession of Merida, driving the chief and headquarters of his army out of this fine old town. It stands on the Guadiana, had a bridge of sixty arches, said to have been built by the Romans, as well as the town, which was partly of very great antiquity. Here we were quartered for some time amongst pretty girls and burly priests, who kept a sharp look-out upon their intimacy with British heretics. This was all jealousy; for I think I had cause to see and believe they were the most immoral and irreligious part of the community. Lazy, indolent, useless cowls, and their name was Legion. The senoritas were generally very pretty, very graceful, ladylike, and extremely correct in manner, morals, and conduct, although at times there was an elopement with some wild handsome young fellow who knew the soft language, which cannot be surpassed in love-making. How many of those poor girls were forced into convents by the aid and advice of crafty priests, where their young hearts were blighted for ever! I often had conversations with them through their iron grating, hearing them wailing and lamenting their unhappy fate, and pining for liberty. 'We are here,' they would say, 'like birds with clipped wings, powerless'; then a little noise perhaps, and they would fly like a chamois, with an '*adios, adios, caballero. Otro tiempo.*'

Monsieur le General Drouet gave us a great deal of bother at this time, marching and counter-marching across that great plain to Almandraleho, a little town some five leagues distant. There he assembled his army, took up position, inviting a quarrel, but always declining to fight. When we got within reach of a nine-pounder gun, he was off in retreat, leaving no chance of giving him a checkmate. Here we halted, generally for a couple of days, and returned to Merida. This game was played so often, I was thoroughly acquainted with every big tuft of grass and swampy pool over that dreary plain ploughed up by wheels, cavalry, and baggage animals. The object of the French was to harass our troops as much as possible, and to keep us away from Ciudad Rodrigo, a great fortress, which he knew would be attacked by Wellington before we could advance up country.

Settled down once more in Merida, *pro tem*, we tried to be happy. I was now pretty well broken into harness, learned something, and began to like my trade, seeing all my comrades as jolly and fearless as if they were foxhunters. We were soon, however, on the trot again. Our division was separated, and placed in different towns and villages near Rodrigo.

In January 1812, Wellington (as I may now call him with great respect) laid siege to Ciudad Rodrigo (city of Rodrigo), and now for the horrors of a siege, and the double horrors of another near at hand; this one lasted twelve days, the city being stormed on the 19th January. Wellington's morning order on that day was laconic and to the point, understood, and nobly responded to; it was this, 'Ciudad Rodrigo must be stormed this evening'.

All the troops reached their different posts after dark; the storming-parties—volunteers and forlorn-hope— foremost; as they advanced they were ravaged with a tempest of grape from the ramparts, which staggered them; however, none would go back, although none could get forward, for men and officers falling fast from the withering and destructive fire choked up the passage, which every minute was raked with grape-shot. Thus striving, and trampling alike upon the dead and wounded, these brave fellows maintained the combat.

The stormers of another division, who had 300 yards of ground to clear, with extraordinary swiftness dashed along to the glacis, jumped into the ditch, eleven feet deep, and rushed on under a smashing discharge of musketry and grape, gaining the ascent; the foremost were blown to shatters, their bodies and brains splashing amongst their daring comrades behind, which only stimulated their determined exertions and doubled their strength. Supports came forward, all the officers simultaneously sprang to the front, when the Herculean effort was renewed with a thrilling cheer, and the entrance was gained. The fighting was continued with fury in the streets, until the French were all killed, wounded, or prisoners; the town was fired in many places; many were killed in the market-place; our soldiers were desperate, really mad with excitement, furious; intoxication, disorder, and tumult everywhere prevailed; discipline and restraint disregarded, the troops committed most terrible deeds. They lighted a fire in the middle of the great magazine, when the whole town would have been blown into the air but for the courage and immediate exertions of some officers and soldiers who were still in their senses, and sensible of the awful gulf around them.

Our loss was, I think, 1,400 soldiers and 90 officers—60 officers and some 700 men fell in the breach. Generals McKinnon and Crawford, two noble and gallant soldiers, were killed; and along with them many stoutly brave fell that day, who feared no danger, and whose lives were more precious than fine gold.

The great obstacle in the advance of the siege was caused by the useless and most disgraceful tools furnished by the Storekeeper-General's office in England. The contractor's profits seemed to be more attended to and respected than our chances of success in taking this fortress.

Three hundred French had fallen, we had 1,600 prisoners, immense stores of ammunition, 150 pieces of artillery, and Marmont's battering train. On the following day, when the escort with the prisoners were marching out by the breach, somehow or other an explosion took place and numbers of both parties were blown into the air!

Wellington was now created Duke of Ciudad Rodrigo by the Spaniards, Earl of Wellington in England, and Marquis of Torres-Vedras in Portugal. Thus ended this chapter of the war.

Chapter Six
Bone Soup

From this time until the middle of March 1812, we were kept roving about the country to pot the French, kill them, and cook them in our own fashion. All was lawful in war, but they were very sharp and always slept with one eye open: we had to do the same. It was like deer-stalking at times—a glorious thing to whack in amongst a lively party with their flesh-pots on the fire of well-seasoned wood. A chest of drawers, perhaps, or the mahogany table of some Hidalgo in the middle of the street blazing away, and the crappos calling out, '*Bonne soupe, bonne soupe*'.

'Bone soup,' says Paddy Muldoon one day, 'those vagabonds live on bone soup: I blive they would make soup out o' an owl gridiron that once fried a red-herrin'. But we're purty near them now, I think, to have a crack at their bone soup.'

Paddy, a front-rank man of the Light Company, was in advance as we cautiously moved along under cover of some of the evergreen olive-trees and stone walls. He was brave, but nervously irksome to be at his work whenever he smelt a Frenchman; and here he spoiled our fun and a capture. As we approached the head of the village, Paddy let fly a shot into the middle of a covey who were in reality cooking their dinner, as I have said. Then a general rush on both sides; one party to grapple their arms and run-the other to pursue, slay, or capture. But the French Light Infantry run very fast when there's powder and lead at their heels, and no blame to them. Paddy was called to account for breaking the peace without orders.

'I couldn't help it, sir, you see, for I had a fine rest for my firelock on the wall, and was sure of one on 'em, bein' in line sitting so close; but they've left their kittles behind, and o' course their bone soup, packs and all.'

We gave them chase a little way, and captured a few, who Paddy said had corns, for the rest got into a wood and cleared out of sight in no time. The kettles were left and examined: some contained bits of pork and vegetables, or a gallina or old hen, but no fresh meat.

"Pon me conscience,' says Muldoon, 'that's the cook I knocked over, for there's the bullet-hole right through his pot, and I'm sorry for him; but he kept a bad look-out.'

This was merely a small advance picket of the French. Such things happen almost every day, and there was nothing more about it.

War for three years was spread over unhappy Spain; battles were fought, men were slaughtered, the country ravaged, houses robbed and burned, families flying to the mountains to escape the horrors of licentious soldiers. The terrors of a marauding army are little known. Legions of low-caste, vulgar men, all loose amongst the people—always for evil, never for good. Then the guerilla bands for ever watching the French, intercepting their convoys and detachments, and pouncing into them from the rocks and mountain passes, dealing fearful death to every victim; and this continued for six years in a charming country, amongst a formerly happy, contented, and amiable peasantry. I have been at the heels of a French party as they escaped from a sweet little country town, leaving their camp kettles on fires in the street, lighted (as I have said) by household furniture, and sometimes one or two members of a family lying murdered on their own hearth-stone! This was but too common a tragedy, and repeated very often to my own personal knowledge.

Chapter Seven
Towards Badajos

We again returned to our quarters at Albuquerque early in March, and I made my acquaintance once more with the look-out tower, where the order was vigilance from dawn to dark.

The British army now began to concentrate their forces in Estremadura. A great battering train was moved up from Elvas, a large fortified town in Portugal, about three or four leagues from Badajos. This was a laborious, slow-coach affair, the great guns were moved slowly along, with only a cavalcade of bullocks the whole length of the natural road that never felt a stone on its soft surface; hundreds of the Spanish peasantry were employed carrying the shot and shell. All the engineers, sappers, and miners were called to attention. Groups of officers at every corner with unusual solemnity talked of the coming storm, when ground would be broken, who were to lead the way, what divisions to be chosen, and who would describe the fall of Badajos to friends at home.

No one doubted the success of the enterprise, but no one ventured to say that his life was his own after the first gun was fired. There was a terrible day approaching, but nobody afraid, even bets being frequently made on the day and hour of the opening ball.

I had no particular nervous feeling now. Men stand together and encourage each other in the hour of danger, but I can't understand the man who would openly express himself callous to all feeling under a shower of lead, or before the mouth of a cannonade. A common saying was, 'every bullet has its billet', and all seemed outwardly serene.

Badajos, which stands on the river Guadiana, in a plain, is about the strongest fortress I had ever seen; but there was nothing proof in those days against British valour. Here were two of the most warlike nations on earth armed against each other in deadly strife, '*Vive Napoleon! vive L'Empereur!*' was the exciting cry on one side; on the other, 'Hurrah for old England'. A flourish of drums, with the 'British Grenadiers' or 'Garryown', set our fellows wild for a dash at any time. Both were so badly armed that I wonder how we killed each other at all. But the distance was very short at times, and the bayonet did a great deal of the work. The French never liked the steel, still, they were brave, very brave.

The days rolled away quickly as they do at present. We got a small advance of pay. The 17th was my birthday, and if I had no salutations, gifts, or a home jollification, I had a good loaf of Spanish bread, a pork chop, and a bottle of country wine, all alone in my billet, and was content. The battalion was so scattered, that few of us Subs could form a little mess to put our rations into the same pot to make some bone soup. My billet was on a very respectable family—the patrone, his senora, and two daughters, both '*hermosa*'. We sat of an evening over the *brazero*, or brass pan, filled with charcoal, red cinders, which kept life in our finger-tips. It was renewed occasionally, and we conversed about the coming storm, for they had many friends in Badajos. I had picked up the language pretty well for my time, which was a great advantage; it is a sweet and expressive language and easily learned.

The Duke had now arranged his plans. Patrick's day came round as usual, and on that fighting festival-morning the band and drums enlivened all Patlanders with the national tune. The same night 1,800 men broke ground 160 yards from the out fort of Picurina, protected by a guard of 2,000; so that some of the Irish soldiers were not altogether disappointed in having a bit of a shindy before they went to sleep. There was a call for some volunteer officers for the engineer department, and to superintend the work in the trenches—two from the 34th—Lieutenants Masterman and George Bell. I was very much attached to poor 'M'; he did me a service once, and I never forgot the smallest kindness in all my career, which has been a long one. The trench work was as dangerous as it was arduous and now the work of death began in reality.

Generals Picton, Colville, Kempt, and Bowes, commanded alternately in the trenches. All the arts of war then known were brought into play on both sides, for the attack and defence. Every man carried his life in his hands; hope lived in the hearts of all. Many were our difficulties. Torrents of rain at nights poured upon the working parties, shot and shell continually striking down the men, provisions scarce, our pontoon bridge carried away, artillery and engineer officers being killed and wounded every day, but no suspension of the fiery trial.

About nine o'clock on the night of the 24th the assault was made on Fort Picurina. The distance was short and the troops quickly closed on their game—black and silent before—now one mass of fire. The depth of the ditch baffled them, also the thickness of the poles. The quick shooting of the enemy, and the guns from the town, rendered the carnage dreadful. Rockets were thrown up by the besieged; the shrill sound of the alarm-bells, mixing with the shouts of the combatants, increased the tumult. Still Picurina sent out streams of fire, by the light of which dark figures were seen furiously struggling on the ramparts, fighting hand to hand with the enemy. None would yield until but 86 men of the fort and the Commandant were left. Our loss was 18 or 20 officers and some 300 men killed and wounded. This was only clearing the way a bit. A frightful and destructive havoc was carried on inside and outside (in particular) the town until the 4th of April. Time being now a great object, and Soult advancing with a large army to relieve the city, the breach being reported practicable, 18,000 of our daring British soldiers burned for the signal of attack.

The assault was arranged and ordered for the next evening, and eagerly did the men make themselves ready for a combat so fiercely fought, so terribly won, so dreadful in all its circumstances, that posterity can scarcely be expected to credit the o'er true tale; but many are still alive who know that it is true.

Chapter Eight
The Assault on Badajos

The night was dry and cloudy, the trenches and ramparts unusually still—lights were seen to flit here and there—while the deep voice of the sentinels proclaimed 'All well in Badajos'. The British, standing in deep columns, as eager to meet that fiery destruction as the French were to pour it down, were both alike, gigantic now in terrible strength and discipline, resolute, and determined to win or die. The recent toil and hardship, the spilling of blood, the desire for glory, an old grudge and a dash of ferocity, not omitting the plunder, the thirst for spoil, and pride of country and arms, caused our men never to doubt their own strength of arms to bear down all before them, and every obstacle opposed to their furious determination. At ten o'clock the Castle, the San Roque, the breaches, the Pardaleras, the distant bastion of San Vincente, and the bridge-head on the other side of the Guadiana, were to have been assailed at the same time. It was to be hoped that the enemy would quail and lose some of their strength within this girdle of fire. But many are the disappointments of war, and it may be taken as a maxim that the difficulties are so innumerable that no head was ever yet strong enough to forecalculate them all.

An unforeseen accident delayed the attack of the 5th Division, as at first intended. A lighted carcass, thrown from the castle, falling near, rendered it necessary to hurry on the attack about half an hour before the time which was subsequently arranged. So, all being suddenly disturbed, the 4th and Light Divisions moved swiftly and silently against the breaches, and the guard of the trenches rushing forward with a cheer, encompassed the San Roque with fire, and broke in so violently that little resistance was made there; but a sudden blaze of light and the rattle of musketry indicated the beginning of a frightful conflict at the castle.

General Kempt fell here wounded; General Sir Thomas Picton took his place. The men dashed forward under a terrible fire, spread and raised their ladders against the castle walls, and with unexampled courage ran up under a shower of shot and shell, stones and small arms, while a fearful fire was kept up on the red-coats from flanks and centre. The leading men on the ladders were met by pikes, bayonets, and musketry, and their ladders pushed from the walls. Now the deafening shouts, crashing of broken ladders, and the shrieking of the crushed and wounded men, became loud amongst the din of war. Excited to madness, the comrades of the undaunted brave below, who swarmed again round the ladders, swiftly ran up, and were tossed over from the enemy above, who cried, 'Victory!' and 'Why don't you come into Badajos?'

The brave Colonel Ridge, with a voice like thunder, called to his men to follow, raised a ladder to the wall a little further off, and met but little opposition until he got in. Another ladder was raised, and our men went pouring in, took the enemy in the flanks, and delivered a volley which very much astonished and staggered them. Here another fight commenced, and here poor Ridge fell— no man died a more glorious death in battle, although multitudes of brave men fell who deserved great military glory.

The frightful tumult at the main breach all this time, the incessant roar of cannon, musketry, bursting of shells, yells of the wounded, and cheering of those who had so short a time to live, rent the air in a fiery lava of exploding shells and barrels of powder.

Every flash showed the French ready and prepared on the ramparts; showed their glittering arms, dark figures, heaps of live shells, and an astonishing amount of artillery, every man having three loaded muskets beside him. Yet our men leaped into the ditch, of whom 500 volunteers, being foremost, were dashed to pieces with shot, shell, and powder barrels. The Light Division stood for a moment in horror at the terrific sight; then, with a wild shout dashed with one accord into the fiery gulf, and, with the light of a blaze of fire-arms from above, the 4th Division followed in an excited fury.

One hundred men were drowned in the inundation (for at this time the sluices were opened, and the water let into the ditch from the river). They now turned off to the left, seeking for the main breach, and got crowded and mixed together. The only light was that of the flashing guns, pouring death and destruction among them.

The confusion was great, but all cheered like thunder; the French cheers also were loud and terrible. The bursting of grenades, shells, and powder-barrels, the whizzing flight of blazing splinters of barrels, the loud voices of the officers, and the heavy groans of the dying, were sufficient to create a terror indescribable.

Now they found the way, and went at the breach like a whirlwind. Sword-blades, sharp and pointed, fixed in ponderous beams, were in their front as they ascended; planks, too, filled with iron spikes; while every Frenchman had three or four loaded muskets at his feet, with leaden slugs over the usual bullet. Hundreds of our men had fallen, dropping at every discharge, which only maddened the living. The cheer was for ever on, on, with screams of vengeance and a fury determined to win the town. The rear pushed the foremost into the sword-blades to make a bridge of their bodies rather than be frustrated in their success. Slaughter, tumult, and disorder continued. No command could be heard; the wounded struggling to free themselves from under the bleeding bodies of their dead comrades; the enemy's guns within a few yards, at every fire opening a bloody lane amongst our people, who closed up, and, with shouts of terror as the lava burned them up, pressed on to destruction. Officers, starting forward with an heroic impulse, carried on their men to the yawning breach and glittering steel, which still continued to belch out flames of scorching death.

About midnight, when 2,000 men had fallen, Wellington, who was looking on, sent an order for the troops to retire and reform for another attack. In the retreat from the ditch there was great confusion and terrible carnage under the continual fire of the French. The groans and lamentations of the wounded trampled on, and expecting to be left to the mercy of an exasperated and ferocious enemy, were awful. Who could explain their feelings? The bitterness of death to them was past. The 3rd Division had gained the Castle. The 5th Division also was engaged at another point. The town was girdled with fire; General Walker's brigade was escalading—the Portuguese troops were unnerved, and threw down the ladders. Our men snatched them up and raised them against the walls nearly thirty feet high. The ladders were short, yet the men clambered up. The fire of the French was deadly; a mine was sprung under the soldier's feet, live shells and beams of wood were rolled over on them with showers of grape; man after man dropped dead from the ladders. Other points were attacked and won.

The French fought like demons. A death struggle of fiery antagonists took place at every corner, while our men most thoroughly maddened with rage and excitement, dashed at the breach with wild resolution: for is it not recorded, 'Who shall describe the martial fury of that desperate soldier of the 95th, who, in his resolution to win, thrust himself beneath the chained sword-blades, and there suffered the enemy to dash out his brains with the ends of their muskets'.

Here now was a crushing and most desperate struggle for the prize; the bright beams of the moon were obscured with powder-smoke. The springing of mines, powder-barrels, flashing of guns and small arms, rendered our men marks for destruction. Death's grasp was just on the remnant of the brave, a total annihilation of humanity on our side, when the troops who had escaladed the Castle made a dash at the breach, and, with one loud cheer for England, and a sweeping volley, and another mad shrieking yell, rushed on with the bayonet, and cleared the bloody gap for those below, who now rushed in, driving the French from every point—and Badajos was won!

Let any one picture to himself this frightful carnage taking place in a space of less than a hundred yards square. Let him consider that the slain died not all suddenly, nor by one manner of death; that some perished by steel, some by shot, some by water, some crushed and mangled by heavy weights, some trampled upon, some dashed to atoms by the fierce explosions, that for hours this destruction was endured without shrinking, and that the town was won at last. Let any man consider this, and he must admit that a British army bears with it an awful power. No age, no nation ever sent forth braver troops to battle than those who stormed Badajos. When the extent of the night's havoc was made known to Lord Wellington, the firmness of his nature gave way for a moment, and the pride of conquest yielded to a burst of grief for the loss of his gallant soldiers.

Chapter Nine
The Sacking of Badajos

For two days the town was in possession of the victorious, and it may be as well to draw a veil over the misdeeds of men stained with the blood of their comrades, now excited to very frenzy. A siege is always terrible, but the sacking of a town is an abomination. Here the inhabitants suffer the terrible vengeance of all the ferocity of the human species.

I remember two sisters, beautiful daughters of Spain, who made their escape from the town when the soldiers spread for plunder and mischief. They made their way into our camp outside, and threw themselves on the protection of the first British officers they met (two of the 95th Regiment). One of those ladies married her protector. I knew them both: he became a distinguished general officer, and now lies in Westminster Abbey; she is still living. Those scenes that took place in the town were frightful, not fit to be recorded. The priests took refuge with the fair sex in the great church for safety, and barricaded the doors. There was no safety anywhere, the maniacs, for the time, loaded their firelocks and let fly a volley into the lock of the door, which opened it quickly enough, and then—

The wine-shops were all in demand. If the men were not all drunk there were none of them quite sober, but very able to go on with the plunder. One fellow might be seen with a bag of dollars; another cove would take him into a wine-house, make him stupidly drunk, and carry off the *douros*; one or two more working in concert would knock this chap down, and rob him of his treasure.

They brought all sorts of things into the camp, until the tents were supplied with furniture such as was never seen in a camp before. One fellow with a tattered red coat, grasping his firelock, was groaning under an old-fashioned eight-day clock; while another had a broad looking-glass on his back; chairs and tables, priests' vestments, ladies' dresses, beds, blankets, and cooking-pots, with sausages, and pig-skins of wine.

'Stop, Jack, and give us a dhrink ov that wine', some fellow would say (dressed in his half-bloody uniform, and on his head the sombrero of an old priest).

'Devil a drop, now; it's going to the camp.'

'Faith an' I'll tapt it for my self, then', and slap goes his bayonet into the skin and out flows the wine. Then there is a wrangle, then they are friends, and both get jolly drunk and lie there helpless long enough.

There were watches amongst them, gold and silver, some valuable ornaments, doubloons, and dollars; they were fond of parading their treasure, and more fond of drinking to excess; consequently these articles changed hands frequently as they got drunk, and the sober ones saved them the trouble of looking after their stolen goods. But still the truth must be told: the besieging army were promised the sacking of the town when taken, and, notwithstanding all the devotion and bravery of the British soldier, this promise of pillage adds to his courage and determination. Therefore it became their reward, and as all the Spaniards in the city had timely notice of the siege, and were offered a free and safe escort away to any place of safety, those who chose to remain stayed at a fearful risk. Very many went away at the beginning, but many who favoured the French party remained to their cost. There was no discipline as yet amongst the stormers; all was riot, confusion, and drunkenness.

The officers had no control over their late devoted and

obedient soldiers; they were mad, and went about with loaded muskets and fixed bayonets, to the terror of each other and everybody else. The Duke rode into the town with his staff, on the evening of the second day, and was immediately recognised.

'There he comes, with his long nose,' said one old warrior who knew him well; 'let's give him a salute.' A dozen or so of half drunken fellows collected, fired a volley of ball cartridge over his head, with a cheer, saying, 'There goes the owl chap that can leather the French!' and then they all cut away and hid themselves out of his sight.

It was rather a dangerous *feu-de-joie,* for the commander-in-chief, who did not seem to like it, went off directly and gave orders for a gibbet to be erected in the great square, and had it proclaimed in camp and through the town that any man found in Badajos the next day would be hanged! This seemed to sober the drunken and curb the passions of all. Fatigued almost to death with fighting and excitement, riot and drunkenness, they were glad of some rest, and, gathered in now to the camp, became obedient to orders, and got ready for any future emergency. Many a bloody, hard-contested battlefield was still before them which I intend, in my poor insignificant way of writing, to record, but only what I saw and shared in.

Badajos had now fallen, and with it 5,000 of our bravest men; and, to the discredit of the English Government, no army was ever so ill provided with the means of prosecuting such an enterprise. The ablest officers trembled when reflecting how utterly destitute they were of all that belonged to real service; without sappers and miners they were compelled to attack fortresses defended by the most warlike, practised, and scientific troops of the age. The best officers and the finest soldiers were obliged to sacrifice themselves in a lamentable way, to compensate for the negligence and incapacity of a Government always ready to plunge the nation into a war without the slightest care of what was necessary to obtain success. The sieges carried on by the British in Spain were a succession of butcheries, because the commonest materials, and the means necessary for their art, were denied the engineers. This liberal and generous Government and their noble successors took thirty-six years to consider whether the men of Badajos and those who fought their way from Torres Vedras to Toulouse, in victorious conquest for six long years, were yet worthy to wear a medal!

Chapter Ten
Chasing the French

Napoleon's troops fought in bright fields, where every helmet caught some beams of glory, but the British soldier conquered under the cold shade of aristocracy. No honours recognising his daring, no despatch gave his name to the applause of his countrymen; his life of danger and hardship was uncheered by hope, his death unnoticed. He endured with surprising fortitude the sorest of ills, sustained the most terrible assaults in battle unnerved, overthrew with incredible energy every opponent, and at all times proved himself to be a soldier worthy of England.

I was greatly surprised at the size of the guns and mortars used in the fortress—some of the latter were wide enough to admit my head and shoulders. Often when the shot and shell fell and exploded in our lines, they left holes wide enough to bury a horse.

The wounded, amongst whom was my friend Masterman, were sent to the hospital at Estramos, in Portugal, established there as the grand depot for sick and wounded; and now we all broke up from before the shattered town, and went our different ways. Soult had made a forced march down country with a great army to relieve Badajos, and got as far as Merida to be just too late, for our people had blown up two arches in the fine old bridge to delay his progress, and on finding, while within hearing of our guns, that the place had fallen, he retired. Lord Hill went back to Merida. We crossed the bridge, it being repaired in a temporary way by our own engineers, the men passing over by files, the baggage animals one at a time, while great caution was used in getting over the guns. It was melancholy to see the two centre arches had gone, but still there were left fifty-eight in glory.

The French army had divided, and so we had to give them chase. We had a variety of marching and counter-marching, stopping here and there in nice Spanish towns, billeting for a week or two, and then off like a shot when in full enjoyment of rest and peace. Zafra, Fuente del Maistre, Malpartida, Caceres, and *otras pueblas*, were familiar to us all, having visited them so often; but still it was a weary and hungry time with most of us. The army was long unpaid, and our credit low. I found favour in the eyes of the brigade butcher, himself a private soldier of my own regiment, who gave us tick for a bullock's head, heart, or liver—sometimes a sheep's head and pluck—until we got our pay. These, to us luxuries, were his perquisites, for three of us were now messing together, adding any little additions that fortune might throw in our way into the camp kettle. There was a positive general order against plunder, and of course no officer would be guilty of such an act. Our rations were short at times, yet we fed the Spanish troops; and their generals purloined the English gold, robbed and plundered, and sold the very arms supplied them by England for their own defence. Yet if a soldier of ours was caught picking up an old hen or duck, or a stray goose, he was at once tied up, and got six dozen. If a very grave offence—such as robbing the person—he was tried by court-martial, and, if found guilty, hanged upon a tree, and no mistake. I remember seeing three soldiers hanged one morning, on the long projecting arm of a cork tree, for robbing some muleteers; men who would have fought to the death in the battlefield. It was a most melancholy and touching sight, as we marched away, to see three red-coats dangling in the air, awaiting the vultures which generally followed on the army.

The Spanish muleteers were the very life and sustenance of the Peninsular war; we could not have existed without them. Everything was conveyed by them for the army—provisions, ammunition, rum, etc. Their patience, hardiness, and fidelity to the British army were remarkable; but, on the contrary, the men high in rank, generals, governors, diplomatists, hidalgos, the Spanish Junta, and Portuguese leaders, such as the ambitious and intriguing Bishop of Oporto—commonly called the Patriarch—the Sousas were contemptible, selfish, cowardly, ignorant, fraudulent, faithless, and cruel. These were the worthies Wellington had to contend against while fighting their battles—always contentious and deceptive.

Our next exploit was to take and destroy the stronghold of Almaraz, a fortress held by the French on the Tagus. General Sir Rowland Hill assembled his corps of the army in and about the fine old town of Truxillo in the middle of May 1812. My regiment happened to be billeted in this city of Pizarro. His birthplace, his house, still a noble building, gave good cover to our soldiers; altogether a likely place to look at for one's dinner; but there was no hospitality. So we determined to get up a big mess dinner for the whole regiment once for all, to celebrate the battle of Albuera! A celebrated sutler, one Tamet, a Turk, always followed our division with a supply of good things, such as English hams, tea, sugar, pickles, and a variety of other luxuries, all at famine prices; but Senor Tamet was a good-natured fellow, and gave some people tick until the next issue of pay, and continued to give credit to those who paid according to agreement. He now furnished our regiment with what we required for our banquet. We selected a pretty spot outside the town, under some cork trees, marked out the size of our table on the green sod, and cut a trench all round. Our legs in the trench, we sat on the ground, with the table in front, but without a table-cloth. This was our arrangement.

We were like schoolboys about Christmas, looking out for a jollification dinner; but all was rough, and nothing at all smooth in these days. However, the 16th of May was to be a day of festivity.

There had been a great many auction sales of late, so many officers being killed at Badajos. It was usual to sell their effects, and remit the amount of sale to the agents at home. In this way most of us got our supply of clothing. I bought a pony saddle and bridle. Always fond of horses, being light in weight and a good horseman, I was now a sort of mounted officer, and a great don in my own estimation. I was in demand for riding races, too, an amusement manly, cheerful, and always present where there is a British army. While preparations were being made for the 16th, which was the following day, we got orders to cook three days' rations, and march the same night! A sad disappointment—no baggage to accompany the division, so that our return was pretty sure, at least that of the living; but of course we were obliged to postpone our dinner *sine die*. Three of us jolly Subs messed together, called the '*Tria juncta in uno*'; and our motto was, *Toujours pret*'. I gave up my pony to carry our three days' prog, tied up in our haversacks, and slung across the saddle, with three distinct orders to my servant to be careful and follow the column and not lose sight of the troops.

We marched away by moonlight; the men slung their arms, to prevent the enemy seeing our line of march and calculating our numbers, for the barrels were bright in those days and might be seen glistening a long way off by moonlight. The daily polishing of the old flint firelock gave the men an infinity of bother and trouble. Rainy days and night dews gave them a rust which was never permitted on parade, as we were more particular about clean arms and powder dry than anything else. We moved on all quiet, the muleteer alone singing a serenade to beguile the passing hour. We marched through rugged mountain passes nearly all the night, halting about every quarter of an hour, in consequence of the many obstacles in front; and at every halt I was fast asleep on the sod, and everybody else also perhaps.

About four o'clock in the morning my regiment was ordered to halt, the rest of the division pushing on, and now Colonel Fenwick explained our plan of attack in a few words. On the top of a mountain, just above, stood the castle of 'Mirabete', garrisoned by 1,000 French soldiers and eight guns, with a rampart twelve feet high; to storm this place by *coup-de-main*, by an escalade in the old style, and as quickly as possible, was our part of the night's amusement.

Volunteers were called for the forlorn hope, and they jumped to the front in a minute, with an officer, Lieutenant Sullivan, at their head. Being myself orderly officer for the day, I was detailed to go in front with the scaling-ladders to place against the walls, a position I considered at the time equal to a wooden leg; but it never can be too often repeated that war, however adorned by splendid strokes of skill, is commonly a series of errors and accidents. We crawled up this steep ascent with great caution and silence; but just as we approached the tower, a solitary shot was fired at the foot of the hill, and the next moment the castle was in a blaze. Luckily for us it was not yet daylight, and that a cloud of mist hung over the castle top. We could not be seen, but the garrison kept up a random fire, all their shot passing over our heads as we lay on the heather.

It was now too late to surprise our friends, as they rather surprised us with their *feu d'enfer*, and so we retired a little way down and got under cover before dawn. There we lay all day waiting for fresh orders. General Hill, top, was discovered, and lay *perdu* with 6,000 men until nearly day light on the morning of the 19th, when he let loose his troops upon Forts Napoleon and Almaraz. Sharp work and severe loss in the escalade, but our men went there to win, the forts were taken and destroyed, guns spiked and sunk in the Tagus, and all material rendered useless. We lost 2 gallant good officers and 180 men, captured 17 officers and 250 men of the French, besides the number killed, one stand of colours, a large amount of ammunition, stores, etc; opened the passage of the Tajo, and went back to Truxillo. When the day closed, my regiment retraced their steps, and joined the main force all safe and sound.

Chapter Eleven
Truxillo

A little thing deranges the best-laid plans. When leaving Truxillo, as I have stated, I gave my servant his orders; he dallied, and kept too far in rear of the column, in company with a groom of General C--, who was leading a spare horse. They missed the turn in the road, dawdled on until they popped on the sentry of an outlying picket, who popped on to them at once. The General's groom was killed, my fellow was unhorsed, the pony ran away and kicked off saddle, haversacks, prog, and all. That single shot awoke up the garrison above, the whole expedition was deranged, and many lives were lost in consequence; but many, too, were saved, for we left the tower and its garrison for another day, and I cannot say that this grieved me very much!

My pony was found, with his bare back. After having countermarched, three of us found ourselves likely to starve for two days, unless that other coves could spare part of their common cold ration. Colonel Fenwick kindly spared me a bit of his cold beef and biscuit to keep me alive, just at a time when a quartern loaf, a pound of ham, and a quart of brown ale would have tempered my appetite while dinner was being prepared! However, we looked joyfully forward to the coming big dinner at Truxillo. We did return victorious, but not to the banquet. Alas! in our absence a foraging party of French dragoons entered the town and carried off all our larder, with all the baggage they could grasp. The wines were overlooked, and, fearful of another foray, our doctor, who had been left behind unwell, got up a ration dinner with a few other friends, took the chair, represented the whole corps, drank to the success of the war, the memory of the brave who fell at Albuera, a safe return to the regiment, and other toasts, until he got so merry he bolted off to a convent to release the nuns like a gallant knight! Many of the fair senoritas he knew were there pining for liberty; but the watchful and wily priests came to the rescue. There was a shindy of course, a few officers of the baggage-guard, who had shared in the toasts, collected their forces and joined the medico. They assailed the convent again, and had nearly forced an entrance, when the second in command received a wound on the head and tumbled down the stairs. The doctor called off his troops to see after the wounded, and dressing the *cabeza* of the only one, made an awkward incision on his *corona*. The *sangre* began to flow, and the holy priests made their escape, satisfied in preserving the dark-eyed maidens from the hands of such heretics, and keeping perdu lest they might get into a scrape for wounding one of H.M.'s officers in uniform. After this quixotic deed the dinner party retired to their *siesta*, and I believe all got up sober.

Great ferocity existed at this time amongst the guerilla chiefs, and indeed at all times. Mina was cruel and revengeful. The curate Merino, too, was revolting in cruelty; he took some hundred French prisoners on one occasion, and, hanged fifty or sixty of them in cold blood, deliberately butchering them in order to avenge the death of three of his men, although he had no proof of their being killed at all. Then there was counter-retaliation, and so the blood work went on continually, both parties to be condemned. Yet, make the case our own, and ask, if an enemy landed on our shores, killed, burned, and destroyed all before them, what would we do? How would we feel towards such an enemy? The poor Spaniards had very great provocation; but still no one could approve of the ferocious conduct on either side.

There was at all times a chivalrous feeling between the English and French in all their quarrels. We respected each other when prisoners of war, and sometimes in deadly strife I have known some instances of such generous conduct. For example: at Elboden there were some days of hard fighting, and some brilliant examples of skill and bravery. In a cavalry charge, a French officer, in the act of dashing sword in hand at the gallant Lieutenant-Colonel Felton Harvey, of the 14th Light Dragoons, saw, just in time, that he had but one arm, and with a movement as rapid as his horse brought down his sword into a salute, and passed on. Nothing on military record more manly, or more beautiful than this!

About this time I was ordered away, in charge of a convoy of sick and wounded, to the grand depot at Estramos, in Portugal. I sold my pony to raise the wind and pay my debts, and prepared for my long journey. I had about ten dollars over, and my donkey, which was now all my own. I bought him out and out; he carried all my world's treasure on his broadside, and might have carried myself at times, for he was not overloaded. An old leather trunk containing my kit on one side, balanced by a sack on the reverse, which held the frying-pan, camp-kettle, reaping-hook, and some odds and ends, with my servant's knapsack, a privilege which he claimed when away from the regiment. Tom Tandy, who was a good forager, always left room in the sack for anything Providence might send on the way, as he said, 'to help the rations'. He drove the Willing donkey before him, and we commenced our journey.

My troop were all mounted on commissary mules, one muleteer having charge of three or four. Taking sick and wounded down to the depots, they always returned to the army with a cargo of rum and biscuit. They were constantly employed.

Chapter Twelve
Campaigns With Quill

My companion, the assistant-surgeon in charge, was a joyous fellow, full of Irish wit and humour, and all sorts of quaint sayings and drollery. His name was Maurice Quill. Any old soldier still in the land of the living, who served in Spain, would remember something about Dr. Quill and his exploits. We marched away from Truxillo without much regret. Quill stated that he had never had a decent dinner since he came into the country, and could not be worse off on the line of march, although he did not consider it his turn of duty for such practice. The weather was very hot, and the marches sometimes long to some town or village, where, according to route, there was to be cover for the night. A billet, with fire and light, was all that we could demand. If the people were kind, and gave us a welcome, we were soon very good friends, and gave them no trouble. This was generally the case; but they seldom attended to one's appetite, and we really had to forage a bit privately about the roadside, it being considered no man's land, not that I remember personally breaking the law, but I believe I may have said to my Sancho:

'How nice one of those ducks, or that little pig, would fit into the sack, and roast for supper at our next billet'. Somehow or another Tom had a magic knack of inviting these innocents in a playful way into his big wallet, for a ride on the outside of a donkey never agreed with them!

We always called a halt about a mile or so from our next resting-place for the night, to look about us and do a little business, to save our patrone any trouble. Tom took out his reaping-hook, stepped into the next field of standing green corn, and bundled up a ration for the gentleman who carried his knapsack. Never forget the poor dumb animal, he must live as well as his master. As for the muleteers, they were at home, and took good care of themselves, and so we snailed along until we came to Badajos, the mutilated and battered old town. They were building up the walls and ramparts, and cleaning away the debris out of the ditches as we passed in. All the tools were laid down as they scanned the cavalcade with sympathy, and with a '*Viva los Engleses*' and '*Via con Dios*'. Having first housed my troops and left Quill to look after their health, I went in search of my billet, and to arrange for our dinner. The great event of the day is a good dinner, here and there and everywhere, with cheerful company, and we fared very well. A gallina and sausages, salad, bread, and good country wine, formed no bad repast after a march of seven leagues. The Spanish bread is the finest in the world, the pork in its season most excellent, and the sausages, with the little tinge of garlic, the best I ever tasted. Quill was very tired with his long tramp, as he called it, and retired early. I was fairly knocked up myself with the march, and a broiling sun beaming on my head all the day. I had comfortable quarters in the square—two rooms and a decent kind of bed. The windows below were all guarded by iron gratings. My bedroom was decorated by an iron balcony, from which I looked out on the poor, desolate, shattered city, hardly a house visible without a smash. Spaniards were still coming in looking for their old habitations, others mending, patching up temporary dwellings, and looking patiently bewildered.

The seven-league march sent me early to roost. Tom picked out a soft plank for himself on the floor outside my door. I left my window wide open to see the dawn and be early away, tumbled in amongst the fleas, and was soon insensible to their claws. I will back Spain and

Portugal against the world for the breed of this very lively creature. Like the dogs in Constantinople, I believe they are encouraged to live and multiply. Always early, I jumped up about five o'clock, rather late for me, and to my horror found nothing in my room but an old shooting-jacket, a pair of trousers to match, my cocked hat and feather, my sword and shoes! I opened the door and found Tom Tandy asleep, gave him a kick to open his eyes, and then asked if he had been in my room.

'No, sir.'

The whole thing now flashed before my eyes, the open window invited some *ladrone* to walk in and inspect my kit. It was easily done, like crawling up a ladder—everything valuable was gone: my trunk and its contents, red coat, boots, trousers, and all—with the few dollars I had in reserve for hard times coming—all this to me just now was a great calamity. I flung myself into the tattered garments left, and ran off to tell the medico, still hoping it might be some trick of his; but, soon undeceived, I related the sad tale, of which he knew nothing, but kept saying, 'I'll get your traps for you.'

When dressed he said, 'Now, come along, and show me your *Patrone*' (landlord). I saw that he was screwing himself up for a charge at the Patrone.

I said, 'He knows nothing of the robbery; Tom was asleep, with his head to my door, all night.'

'Never mind, I must see him.'

I sent Tom down for the senor. As soon as the poor gentleman appeared, the doctor made a spring, and fastened in his collar, saying, in his own native language and excitement, 'If—you—don't—get—this—officer—all—his—things—which—you—stole—I'll—cut—your—(Spanish)—throat'. laying an emphasis on every word, that the Spaniard might not misunderstand him!

The poor man was dreadfully alarmed. There was a noisy row. His daughter, a pretty black-eyed maid, rushed in to the rescue, at the time the doctor was making signs of an incision across her father's throat. I tried to drag him off; the young lady screamed, but the medico declared it was all sham, and he would have my traps restored. However, I got the senor released from an iron grasp, and his daughter in tears took him away.

Quill at the same time took his leave, saying, 'If I chose to submit to be robbed at every billet in Spain, not to call upon him for any advice or assistance!'

He could not speak a word of Spanish, and was much prejudiced against the whole race, believed every man in the country to be a public robber, and looked sharp after his own kit. He was not very far wrong, but still there were honest men and women too, and plenty of them, who loved '*los Engleses*' as well as their own bright land.

Time being nearly up, I ran off to the office of the Alcalde to report my misfortune, not expecting much redress there.

'Give me a list of your losses,' he said, 'and I will make inquiry after them. You must wait the result here.'

I gave him the list in writing, and my address, name, regiment, and division of the army, and there it ended. Going back with all my dander up and a melancholy phiz to move off my traps, I heard a sweet voice from a balcony call out, 'Senor George'. I looked up, and saw a fair lady whom I had known formerly in my old quarters at Albuquerque.

She called me up, and, quite rejoiced to see me again, asked a hundred questions all at once. Where was the regiment? How were all the officers? How came I here in this queer dress? And where I was going? When she gave me time to speak I told her all, which greatly distressed her.

'To be robbed,' she said, 'amongst my own people'; and, '*Dios mio, yo siento mucho,*' etc., and 'I'm grieved that I cannot help you. I am only here to see some friends who stood out the siege; we are all poor now. Our property destroyed and pillaged, and Spain ruined. You must have some chocolate and something to eat by the way, and two of my brother's shirts, and—'

"Oh, no,' I said, 'I can't take anything. I must be off, my people are waiting.'

But the chocolate came in with some toast, the *almuerzo* (breakfast) of all the better class of Spaniards. I parted from her with great reluctance, and with what is called a tender good-bye too. She saw me to the door, slipped two dollars into my hand, and ran upstairs with a '*povorasito*' on her lip, and a '*viva mil anos, caro amigo, a-Dios.*' Dear, sweet, gentle, kind-hearted Leonora! I never saw her afterwards to return a hundred-fold her generosity. I would have walked a long day's journey to have met her again to show my gratitude—so much was I touched with this disinterested loving-kindness.

I found my troops all present, and in the saddle—'a pack-saddle'. 'Nobody dead, sir,' said the medical officer and took his usual place in front. Away I went from Badajos in very light marching order, never to see it again. The doctor was as mute as a tombstone for two leagues, when I called a halt, and sat down by the side of a clear nice fountain, while the mules had their refreshing beverage. Quill now came up and sat down beside me, with a laughing face and admonition for not permitting him to 'choke that rascally Spaniard who stole my traps'.

'I hope he didn't steal the frying-pan.' 'I have all the cooking traps,' says Tom, who was sitting beside his donkey at the fountain, gnawing a bone.'

'All,' says the doctor—'a tin pot and an ugly frying-pan.'

'All we want, sir,' said Tom, 'where nothin's to be got without money, and I haven't seen a dollar of my pay for five months, and nuffin' to eat but the rations.'

'What are you eatin' now, then?' said Quill.

'Just pickin' a sheep's wag, sir, I got at the last billet.'

'Or the hotel, say, where you paid for everything, and two sheep and a pig into the bargain.'

'Sir, you're hard upon the *patrone*. He couldn't get into master's room, yer see, the door being shut and my head up again it all night. It was some ladrone that climbed up and got in at the window, which was wide open and easy as a stair. They're not bad people the Spaniards, sir, if you could speak to them like me, sir, and not meddle with anything about their doors. You see, sir, when the old fox wants a goose or a duck, he always goes away from home to forage, and never touches a chicken near his own den.'

'*Vamos, senor*,' said the leading muleteer, and we moved on.

The doctor came up to me and said that he had a few dollars in his pocket, and would divide with me the last pisetta, and made himself very agreeable until we crossed the border and entered the little kingdom of Portugal, put up at Elvas, a strongly fortified town. We met an officer, Lieutenant Bowers, of the 50th stationed there, an old acquaintance, and passed the day with him. I had no occasion, I said, to lock my door tonight, for all my wardrobe was on my back, which astonished a well-dressed military officer of the British army, until I explained the cause.

'Why,' he said, 'if you were not so very young, you would be taken for some guerilla chief, and all the convoy for prisoners of war, only that the guerillas are on our side.'

'Just so,' I said, 'and that makes all the difference.'

We passed on our way without any adventure until we sighted Estramos, the end of our journey. It was a bright sunny day, hot as you please. About noon, as I headed my long line of mules bearing the lame, and the sick, and the sore, the battered trunks of brave men representing many corps, a general officer and his staff, with their cocked hats and fine plumage, stood in the middle of the square and caught my eye at once, as I marched in at the head of my troop. With open mouth and eyes they all turned towards this spectacle, particularly the commanding officer in the fancy dress. Up comes an aide-de-camp directly from the General, to inquire who I was, where I came from, my name, 'and about your dress, sir'. I thought I would have a rise out of the well-dressed gentleman, so sleek and so well fed.

'Just from the fighting army above,' I said. 'We are not over particular in dress; hard times too, little to eat, and plenty of field exercise in the fire-away-style; here's a sample of our trade behind me.'

He went off to make his report to his master, who sent him back for a more direct reply, particularly about my uniform. I then told him the whole story, and my duty being discharged when I had delivered my troops at the general hospital, requested permission to proceed to Lisbon to get a new rig out.

The General gave me two months' leave at once, but forgot to ask me to dinner! Quill wished me a safe return through Badajos, and desired me to be sure to call and apologise to my old patrone! And ask him for my toggery, particularly the *douros*! We shook hands and parted mutual good friends—more of him again.

I went in search of my good friend Masterman who had been wounded in the siege; he was nearly recovered. I passed the day with him. He gave me an old military blue coat and two dollars, all he could spare, and with this

I began my journey over a whole kingdom on foot. Tom had his red coat, so we could not be mistaken for any other than true British soldiers. I knew that there were bandits on the road, but consoled myself with the truth that they would not disturb a couple of English red-coats, driving an empty donkey before them. Tom had his brown bess, and sixty rounds of ball cartridge. He kept his flint well fixed and his powder dry. We had a ride on the donkey, and carried the gun turn about. I was commanding officer and Tom as respectful as on parade, while sober. The first night on our new line of march he got right jolly on wine. He had no money nor credit, but a winning way at the wine-house, and a singular way when he lost his balance. I found him in heavy marching order, firelock in hand, when I thought him in bed for the night.

'Ho, Tom,' I said, 'where are you going?'

'Back to the regiment,' he said. 'I go no further: no service on this road.'

I gave him a punch that floored him right into his little den, where he lay as quiet as a turtle until I took away his gun, knapsack, and ammunition, then locked him up a close prisoner till morning, when he turned out quite fresh and as penitent as priests, who'll never do it again until the next time! And so Tom worried me all the way, but only at night, when I usually locked him up. I had no other adventure on this line of march. Rations were provided by the head man of the village to all who had a route to show, and were paid afterwards by our Commissary.

Chapter Thirteen
Dining with Madmen

It was a long, weary, hungry walk over a little kingdom, but I had a stout heart then, a pair of very active legs, an iron constitution, an appetite too big for my means, a devil-me-care way of my own, always merry and ready for any sort of fun or frolic. I rejoiced to see 'Aldea Gallego'.

Here I crossed the Tajo, nine miles to Lisbon, and made my way to Belem, the English depot, where an officer of my own regiment was stationed. Lieutenant R--n was a kind, hospitable fellow, glad to see me and to give me a room in his quarters, as well as a hearty invitation to be his guest while I remained in Lisbon. I did enjoy myself full measure here; very opportunely, too, a box of clothing had just arrived in the river for me from home, with a permission to draw for the ready; in addition, I was now all right again, and went to work quietly to equip myself out like a campaigner for rough days before me. I got up a canteen, bought a silver spoon and fork, a new frying-pan, tin plates and dishes, and tins for salt, pepper, tea and sugar, etc. A tailor made up my uniforms, riding-jacket, and cap for racing, and other habiliments.

All this was going on while I was enjoying myself. I had a good horse to ride, and dined out often; old starvation ration days were forgotten, and I became a great swell. At this time our old friend, Dr. L—, who played the part of Don Quixote at Truxillo, arrived in bad health, with a home certificate for six months' leave. He came out to dinner with us one day, when we observed by his singular manner that he was not just all right in his pericranium. Dinner was being prepared and wine on the table. He walked in, and was helping himself to a goblet of sherry, when I interposed and requested him to wait a little. He put down the decanter, took up a carving-knife, and made a rush at me. I ran round the table, he after me, when I jumped out of the window, which fortunately was open, and made my escape. I turned round and spoke to him. He flourished his *cuchillo* and told me not to come back, or he would stop my promotion! We found that the poor fellow had gone a little crazy. He had cut half the tail off his red coat, and had played some queer pranks in Lisbon. We had him carefully looked after, and I saw him safely on board a ship and placed under the special care of the captain, who took him safe to England. He was considered a very clever man in his profession. He never rejoined the regiment.

Major B— of ours was promoted into the 77th Regiment, now only seven miles from Belem. He asked us to dine at the mess which they had established. We rode over to have a jollification, for it was almost necessary at that period to drink wine for three hours after dinner; then supper, and finish off with spiced wine and stirrup cup. I saw that my friend R— was getting top-heavy, very loquacious, speaking like a senator, and getting very valiant. He was invited to a shake-down for the night. Oh, no! his gallant grey was at the door and would take him home in no time; so we mounted and rode away quietly about one o'clock in the morning. We had not gone far when my companion fancied he saw a regiment of French Dragoons in his front, and ordered me to charge. He dashed away at full speed, swaying from side to side in the saddle, so that the right or left spur was always in the flank of the poor horse. The moon was bright, and the perfume along the hedges sweet as honey. Such a climate at that hour was meant for the thoughtful, the gentle, thankful, weary traveller on some errand of mercy, not for Don Quixote and Sancho. I am sure if R— had met a windmill in his flight he would have made the fatal charge; as it was, I found him in a ditch by the roadside about a mile on, and his horse standing gently beside him. I jumped off my nag and roused him up. Finding no bones broken, I got him once more into the saddle after a great struggle, for people in their cups are always very wise and very obstinate! No sooner firmly seated than he gave one wild whoop and was off again, full speed. No use in following, I thought; it would only urge on his horse the faster. I rode on quietly, watching both sides of the road for this wild fellow, but never saw him or his horse. I arrived at home about six o'clock in the morning and sent his servants in search of him along the road that we came; but no tidings until midday, when he came riding home quite jolly, as if nothing had happened, and blew me up for leaving him alone in a *quintal* Poor R-- was a very sober fellow at all times, but addicted to gambling, which ultimately ruined him.

I had no desire to dine out again with such-like hospitable friends. A simple repast under a tree suited me better, and I do not remember being at any sort of a mess dinner again during the war.

I saw a good deal of Lisbon this time and the beautiful country around it. As for the city itself at that period, it was the most filthy town I had ever seen: it was dangerous to walk the streets by night. No end to the slops coming from the top windows whop into the gutters below. The dogs were ever on the alert at night, prowling and fighting—a community of scavengers without owners, rejected and kicked about; existing in mangy wretchedness, and dying in the streets. As for beggars, they were as plenty as paving-stones. Lazy, indolent, and filthy, they lay on the hot flags, stretching out the long bone of an arm for an alms, but would not rise for it. They lived in the sun, half-naked; but as a shirt and trousers were quite enough for any *senor Englese*, they required few garments—it was awfully hot.

Chapter Fourteen
Salamanca

My time was now up, and we started—a large detachment of many corps—to join the army. I got charge of a spare horse going up to a field officer of the 2nd Division, so I was in luck. Tom and the donkey in good feather and high condition for the road. Tom was two months under garrison discipline, and sober as a judge; and very glad, as he said, to go home again. We halted at Elvas en route.

I called on the Commandant, and found that officer, dressed in part of my late wardrobe. I said to him, 'Might I ask who is your tailor?'

'Why do you ask?' he said.

'Oh, just because he made for me as well, and my things fit you so nicely. That silk riding-jacket is mine; I had it for riding races. I can't swear to the trousers, but the vest I would know anywhere.'

He seemed very much taken aback, and explained how he had bought several things ready-made from a travelling pedlar, which no doubt was the fact. When I explained the Badajos tale, it was all clear that the pedlar was the *ladrone* (thief), and he had purchased stolen goods, not knowing that they were stolen from Ensign G. Bell, when in the performance of his duty in the service of King George III, of gracious memory. He offered to restore all he had at half the price he paid for them, but I declined his offer, saying that I had a full kit, and really wanted for nothing. Between this little unexpected surprise and excitement he forgot to ask me to dinner, so we parted, and never met again. I was satisfied that I did not awake when the wretched thief was in my room, or I might have felt the plunge of his *cuchillo* under my fifth rib, to keep me quiet. I got home safe, and was welcome. There was no fighting in my absence, so I lost nothing.

I found my young friend P—, who used to drink more than his allowance of grog on board the *Arethusa*, missing, and was informed that, on one unlucky morning for him, the brigade was roused up suddenly to disperse some advance troops of the enemy, who were poaching upon our grounds. They were being followed up close by the infantry when the word was passed to the rear to send up the guns, as they were rattling past, and our men closing to the left, poor P— lost his balance, tumbled over, and a gun-carriage ruffled his legs, with one of the colours in hand. There was an inquiry, and it could not be denied that he had been indulging as usual in too much of the strong waters, so he got leave to go home for an indefinite period, which meant to say that his military career was at an end.

The other gentleman, Lieutenant S—, was found one night while on duty mortal drunk, and got leave to quit also. It was this unfortunate fellow who chased me up on deck with knife in hand for cutting him down on board the old transport.

Commanding officers had almost unlimited power in those days to dismiss officers without court-martial for grave offences like the above. It saved a great deal of trouble and inconvenience, and kept young fellows and old ones *in terrorem*. The men were being flogged every day for drunkenness, and it was right that there should be no partiality between officer and soldier for this crime.

Wellington about this time ordered Sir Rowland Hill to give battle to Drouet, Count D'Erlong, who was roving about our part of Spain with a large army, feeding and foraging upon the unhappy Spaniards, who received nothing but blows and abuse for feeding their enemies.

We hunted them all over the country, and from town to town, but they would not have our acquaintance on any terms. We drove them from Toledo and Valladolid, two cities of Spain celebrated in story. I did so enjoy a short stay in the former. The French were hardly gone when we marched in, and the same evening a ball was given at the Palace in honour of the English General and his officers, the first British troops that had been here. These Spanish balls and parties are not attended with any expense beyond the refreshment of country wine, lemonade, and cakes. The Bishop was present. Many *grandees*, poor and proud, assembled there, and the gentle *senoritas*, so neatly and so simply dressed, looked pensive and beautiful. They move about in the dance so gracefully, while generally their feet and figures are perfect. There is a very fine cathedral here, and a magnificent organ, on which I helped to perform a grand piece of church music in the way of blowing the bellows—a simple process. 'Tis not done by hand, but by the feet. You walk up and down the great double bellows behind the organ. As one exhausts, the other fills, and so 'tis a walk up and down hill while the music lasts. Toledo was celebrated for sword-blades, as it is now for priests and friars. It stands on the Tagus, in New Castile.

We started in chase once more, and they led us a dance at their heels into Leon, declining to enter into any personal gun-powder quarrel with us for the present. We had very long marches and very hungry soldiers, no money and no credit, six months now in arrears of pay, the muleteers twelve. What could one expect in the trail of a French army? I paid 6s. for a loaf of bread, my daily pay being 5s. 3d., less income-tax! Soldiers without money become robbers almost everywhere; but our men behaved admirably. Bad ones were to be found in every corps, because we got the sweepings of jails at home to fill up our ranks, recruits were so scarce at eighteen guineas bounty. But they were all game cocks at fighting; never was such an army, and Wellington knew it.

At this period, our noble Duke and the French General Marmont were dodging each other, and manoeuvring about Salamanca both on the *qui vive* some days before the 22nd of July 1812, on which day the great row began. The battle was fought and won by the noble army of Old England—a day of victory garnished by the blood of thousands. Many a time that day did the battle change its very doubtful position. Wellington was here and there and at every point at the right time. The men went down by hundreds, but won their way by desperate courage through such a fire as British soldiers can only sustain. Onwards they pushed through gloom and blood and powder smoke, which rolled along the field, and clothed the scene in partial darkness. In sounds of terror, the battle raged, volley following volley with deafening rapidity, while charges of cavalry and the booming of great guns swept off the warriors, on both sides brave and bold. They fell in sections, crying victory before the fight had half begun. The French reserve came quickly on upon our front and flanks; their great masses closed on us in clouds of smoke and stream of fire. The hill-side was soon covered with the dead and dying. The battle-ground was shaking like an earthquake, for the French rapidly followed up their advantage, and their fire sparkled along the line with terrible effect, as the many gaps in our ranks clearly showed. The crisis was at hand, and victory awaited the general who had the best and largest reserves.

The 5th Division now met the enemy with a shower of leaden hail in their teeth, a cloud of dust blinded their vision, and in that cloud a tremendous charge of cavalry, swift and sure, sword in hand, broke in upon them in full tilt, trampled and cut them down. They lost both nerve and courage, and upwards of 1,000 men threw down their arms, while the glittering swords of our heavy dragoons, all powerful, cut down all before them; but not before a hundred saddles or more were emptied by a flank fire. The French left was now broken, Marmont was wounded, and some of his Generals, amongst others Desgraviers, killed, the batteries still ploughing through each other's ranks. On our side a sheet of flame advanced in front, men only thinking of victory. A few more desperate conflicts took place along the lines. The French, drunk with excitement, staggered, were beaten, and having lost 2,000 prisoners, retreated in the dusk of evening. With our dragoons at their heels, they made for the Tormes, and crossed that river by night. The Duke, always wide awake, left the Spanish General Carlos d'Espana at Alba de Tormes to intercept the French in case of retreat; but, as usual, he paid no respect to his orders. He left his post, and so let the defeated enemy escape across the ford! Trifling actions often mar great combinations. If this valiant Spaniard had obeyed his orders, at least a third of the fugitives would have been captured. As it was, the victory was great and decisive. Many stories might be told of noble deeds of valour done that day, every tale a true one—of how the gallant soldiers of 1812 fought for Albion, and sent their laurels home.

A 43rd man, shot through the thigh, lost his shoes in the marshy ground. Refusing to quit the battlefield, he limped on under fire with naked feet and blood streaming from his wound, and thus marched on for several miles over a country covered with a small flinty stone.

Kit Wallace, a private in my company, a simple sort of fellow, who had no friends, and was always a butt, and often called a coward in joke, said, 'I'll not fire a shot, a single shot in the rear rank' (his proper place), and rushed to the front, expended his sixty rounds of ball-cartridge, and calling for more, said, 'Now, am I a coward?'

A man who fought beside Wallace was struck with a ball that passed through his body on the right side: you might have put a ramrod complete through the hole. He deliberately took his last shot, walked to the rear, lay down under a tree, and went to sleep in death.

The delicate and beautiful wife of Colonel Dalbiac braved the dangers and privations of two campaigns with the fortitude and patience of her sex. In this battle of Salamanca, forgetful of herself, supported by strong affection for her gallant knight, irresistibly impelled forward, trembling at the fear of death, she rode amidst the enemy's fire, exposing herself to imminent peril. There was no man present that day fighting the battles of his country that did not fight with more than double enthusiasm seeing that fair lady in such danger on the battlefield.

Wellington was hit by a spent shot in the leg, but pushed on early next day after his friends, when there was another row and some slaughter. Poor General Forey had died of his wounds, and was buried by the roadside. The brave Spaniards found the spot, and tore up his body from his humble grave to mutilate and dishonour the shattered shell, when our soldiers came up, and rescued it from their unholy grasp, buried it afresh, and covered it over with large stones for greater safety.

The French lost in this day's sport: 1 Field-Marshal, 7 Generals, 12,500 officers and men killed, wounded, and taken prisoners, 2 Eagles, several standards, and many guns (when we talk of guns we always mean cannon). We lost 6,000 killed and wounded, with 4 Generals. Our troops marched 150 miles in twelve days, just before the battle. Some regiments suffered severely; but the 11th and 61st could not muster at the end of the fight over 150 or 160 officers and men—all that were left to tell of noble deeds done on that hot day. Some 6,000 men lying in the hospitals of Salamanca, besides French prisoners also suffering from their wounds, rendered it the abode of extreme misery. Officers sold their horses and what they could get a few dollars for to sustain life, and many died of want and wounds—in plain language, starved to death from neglect, the reward of devotion and courage unequalled in the annals of Great Britain!

There was no getting quit of these Frenchmen. They multiplied and formed new armies, always on the trot, like locusts, eating up all before them. The order of the day with them was free quarters. They paid for nothing, and it was always an unlucky time for us when we got in their wake, for they cleared out the whole country as they went along, the poor Spaniards hiding out of sight all they could put away. Supposing a brigade of French troops on the march to a certain town, where they would arrive on the next day: they sent an armed escort in advance to the alcalde, or head man there, desiring rations to be ready for, say 500 or 1,000 men next day. There was no alternative but that of providing for these plunderers, or taking the chance of their being let loose to help themselves. 'Ye gentlemen of England, who sit at home at ease', how would you like such visitors along the coast of Kent, or in your snug little country towns?

Chapter Fifteen
Routed Out of Yepes

We passed nearly the month of September in the pretty town of Yepes. It was the vintage season, and all were busy gathering in most delicious grapes and making their wine. The people were very kind, simple, industrious, and happy. My regiment and the 28th were the first British troops that had ever paid a visit here, and we were welcome. The town was divided between the two corps for their separate quarters in this way: the Quartermasters went on in advance, looked into each house, and chalked upon the door, 'Grenadiers, 34th, ten men', more or less according to size and convenience, and so on until the whole corps was disposed of. All this was done without asking the proprietors a single question. The best of the houses were marked for the officers, one or more in each house, as there was room. The commanding officer had the best quarters, of course, and went there at once. When the men were put up, all the officers assembled to choose their quarters by seniority. They were not particularly choice when my turn came. Once in possession, good or bad, no one's senior could turn you out if you selected your house according to regulation.

I had an excellent quarter (that had been overlooked) as far as rooms went. My *patrone* was one of those old *grandees* of Spain, advanced in age, as well as his *senora*. I very seldom saw them, but the servants had orders to look after my comfort, which they did in their own way. My table was served with grapes and sweetly-preserved melons. A loaf of bread and a big sausage would have been more in my way, but I fared better than usual. There were many pretty girls in the town, all fond of dancing, in which we often indulged of an evening, until we became almost as one family. In fact, every young fellow had his sweetheart. The young ladies were charming, barring education. The priests took care to keep them in ignorance, and free from the trammels of overmuch learning, so that they were generally very idle, but fond of music, dancing, gossiping, and eating grapes and chocolate. However, we thought our fair friends here of a superior race, and indulged them in every way we could. It was a terrible blank to those who could not speak their beautiful language.

Our little evening dancing parties were not expensive; lemonade, fruit, and cakes was the usual refreshment—all that we could afford, all that was expected. I was a great *don* in the dance; knew all the figures and all the *bonitas*.

The weather was beautiful, and after morning parade we had nothing to do but enjoy life in this paradise. With my rations and half a cow's head once a week I made out a living.

I walked into the coach-house one day to look at two curiosities in the shape of the Spanish carriage of the olden times. I found on the seat of my host, the *grandee*, a hen's nest with seven eggs, which I put by for breakfast, leaving a white stone in their place, which the good old hen was kind enough to consider sufficient security, and called there every second day.

Wellington all this time was laying siege to Burgos, and although not so strong as Badajos or Rodrigo, he was obliged to abandon it after thirty-three days' pounding and five assaults, with a loss of more than 2,000 men, thanks to the home mis-government not supplying him with the guns he asked for and required. Surprising difficulties met this great warrior at every corner in his every-day arrangements, while straining every nerve to accomplish the very work cut out for him by an English Cabinet. He was always active, vigorous, firm in all his arrangements, with a wonderful foresight and conception, admirably formed for success. But he must have found a certain bad Government a scourge with a double thong. What a man of patience and perseverance!

This failure at Burgos knocked all our charming little arrangements to bits. We thought we had taken root in Yepes, being nineteen days undisturbed.

An unexpected order came to 'march tomorrow'. It came as an order never came before—most unwelcome. All was now hurry and bustle, to get the donkeys ready, and go and see our *hermosa* Castilian maids, and feel there was a farewell to peace and pleasure whilst a Frenchman remained in Spain. My washwoman, Mrs. Skiddy, came in with my two shirts, etc.

'No money yet, Mrs. Skiddy. I owe you a long washing bill.'

'Och, never mind that, jewil, if you never paid me. Sure, you're always mindful of Dan on the march, and carry his firelock sometimes a bit when the crather's goin' to drap wid all the leather straps on his back, and nearly choked wid that stock round his thrapple.'

'Well, we march tomorrow, and so go and get ready.'

'O worra-worra, march the morrow, and not a shoe on me wee donkey. The curse o' the crows be on the French; may they nivver see home,' and away she went, storming agin the French.

When the unwelcome news spread over the town, the young ladies seemed to feel it most, and many of them, indeed, sadly grieved. However, we got up a dance the same evening, as a farewell party. I well remember it was not so joyous as usual. Before the evening was over, many a sigh and gentle tear was heard and seen sliding over pale cheeks. I passed very little of my time in the house of my *grandee patrone*. I was welcome in another quarter, and my comrade and self promised our fair friends to come back and see them from Aranjuez (pronounced 'Aranwhays').

In the early morning the windows were crowded with our sweet young friends. *'Adios, senores! adios, Via con Dios!'* was heard till far away. I believe there were some very tender partings, for we never left a town in Spain with such regret. Our march was over a plain, about six leagues, to the nice town of Aranjuez, on the Tagus, where the country palace of Spanish kings has stood for centuries. Fine gardens and pleasure-grounds, and fishponds and statuary adorned this royalty. Inside the palace all those charms in which kings and queens luxuriate. We had permission to see everything. One room was occupied by mirrors from top to bottom, in which, if any person was shut up, he could never find his way out, so curious was the construction. Another room had its walls entirely covered with paintings—the exploits of Don Quixote, and so on.

A few days passed here, when three of us young fellows agreed to go over to Yepes next morning at daylight, to pass the day, and see our young lady friends once more, according to promise. I was at my post in good time. There was a rumour of a move, and so my two coves backed out of the trip to Yepes. Nothing daunted, I started off alone, and found a joyous welcome after my long walk across a burning plain. My dress was a scarlet jacket and white waistcoat—the Spaniards liked it, and I did not care a rush who did not. I made for the Caza Don Chaves, and ran upstairs without ceremony. There was a great welcome, and, I believe, some kisses, and a hundred questions about *Senor* S. and twenty others, and why they did not come, etc., etc. I was almost swallowed up with kindness. Maria sat before me, with her raven hair so nicely turned back from her snow-white forehead, her ivory teeth seen through her smiles, and her beautiful speaking eyes, listening to all

I said so imperfectly. All the people in the town seemed to be attached to our men, who behaved so well amongst them. They understood each other by a few words and more signs. An early dinner was being prepared, I was in the midst of enjoyment, and going to pay another visit, when some one came rushing in, in great fear, saying, '*Los Franceses! los Franceses! O. per Dios, Senor George,*' (The French are coming! For God's sake, escape for your life—we are all ruined). Another messenger—'*La caballeria, la caballeria viene!*'

All was now hurry, scurry, and excitement in the house to secure valuables, and hide themselves. I tried to compose the ladies by an assurance that they were safe, but their fear of the French, of whom they heard so much, gave them great alarm, and they would not be comforted. I have found ladies in general everywhere much alike in this respect, and I might add that the civillest person I ever met was a woman in a fright. A hasty '*Adios, caras amigas*', and I bolted out of the house—just in time, for the advance guard of a cavalry regiment sounded a halt at the top of a long street leading down to my friend's *caza*. In any other dress than a red jacket, I might have approached near enough to count their numbers and make a report, but my object now was to run for it and escape. I went off at a good round trot for a league or so, and then, wet as a sponge, broke into a smart walk. I might be seen at any distance on this wide plain, and kept both eyes open. Here I met a *pizanno* going to Yepes with a mule laden with wine. The wine in Spain is carried in pigskins, tanned, dried, and prepared lor the purpose, as in days of old Bible history (*Matthew ix. 17*). The bottles might have contained ten or twelve gallons each. I stopped to tell him the news, which seemed to stagger him exceedingly. He knew very well that the French were not in the habit of paying for their wine, nor drinking to the health of the Spaniards.

The salutation of our allies, I well remember, was always, '*Viva los Engleses*'.

He said, 'Is there any of your army in Yepes?'

'None,' I Said, 'I am the last to leave,' and explained as well as I could.

'*Lo siento mucho, senor,*' he said, and began to open a bottle, the mouth of which was a leg of the skin, tied by a string. He had a tin measure, and filled me a bumper. 'Drink', he said, 'you seem hot and tired.' I did with gusto toss off a pint of his *brueno vino,* and bid him God-speed.

I got home just in time to join my regiment crossing the Tagus—one bridge on fire, and the other about to be blown up—a little later, and I should have been on the wrong side! The two bridges had not been destroyed more than an hour or so when the French cavalry approached and sent their videttes down to the river to look after our locality. It might have been very inhospitable, but they received a very ugly discharge of musketry from our riflemen, who lined the banks under cover of the evergreen shrubs and bushes. I was in no good humour with them myself for routing me out of Yepes. So I paid into them some shots from a rest which, I fear, told what I intended at the time, although of all the sports in the field that of man-shooting I like the least. There was a good deal of pot-shooting across the water from our amateurs out of sheer spite, for we were all very angry at being disturbed from our royal quarters. Our troubles were only beginning, but we were in happy ignorance of all before us.

Chapter Sixteen
To Madrid

When night came on, we all moved off silently from before Aranjuez, across some newly-ploughed lands, wherein I sank to the ankles until my short boots got full of sand and dirty water. When we did get into the Camino Real, or 'royal road', there was a halt to let all stragglers come up. Fires were soon lighted and blazing bright. I pulled off my Wellingtons and my socks to get them quickly dry, and fell asleep, so dreadfully tired as I was after the long day's work. I never awoke until the whole army had moved away, and there I was all alone in the darkness of solitude. The fire had nearly burned out. My socks were pretty dry but the boots very damp. I pulled one on after a painful difficulty—the other foot would not go home on any terms. Half on and half off, I limped on until I came up with my regiment at the next halt, fairly knocked up, but continued on till morning, when we pulled up at Madrid.

There, on the bridge leading into the great city, I dropped like a stone, where I lay for two hours unable to move, footsore and weary. The day was fine, and a general rush was made into the town, when the bugles sounded the assembly.

A general order was issued to serve out three days' rations and have them cooked immediately, and then to be ready to march at a moment's warning. The butchers were very expert at their trade. The oxen and fatlings (without any fat) were slaughtered, cut up, divided, served out, and in the camp kettles in less than two hours.

I dragged myself down to the river, got off my boots, washed my socks, got up a fire, and fell asleep. Tom roused me up with, 'The rations, sir.'

'What have you got, Tom?'

'Somewhat of three pounds of beef with a big bone in it, orders to cook and be off again—sharp. I suppose them *Franceses* are coming after us—the d--l's luck to them!'

If my feet sometimes failed me my appetite never did. The dinner was not at all inviting when turned out on a tin plate, but it was all gone in twenty minutes, barring the bone, and I got up rather hungry, and put two pounds of the biscuit into my haversack for the next two day's subsistence.

Fancy being in Madrid without a dollar in one's pocket to buy a loaf of bread or a sausage—all that I desired or cared for at that moment. However, I was now refreshed. The bugles sounded, I rolled my blanket, strapped it on my back, and waited for the assembly call, when the 88th Regiment, or Connaught Rangers, passed by as merry as larks, singing and cracking their Irish jokes. They were regular bronze fellows, hard as nails, and as ready for a fight as for a ration of rum. One fellow took a side glance at me and said, not in a very undertone, 'I think that young gentleman would be better at home with his mother!' I was very indignant at this remark and kept it to myself. I knew they were a crack regiment, and esteemed them for their remarkable bravery at all times.

In Madrid was a junction of the whole British army. Soult and his best Generals were at our heels with 58,000 fighting men, 84 guns, and 8,000 cavalry, a sad turn of affairs as we all thought at the time. So began the grand retreat from Burgos and Madrid; a frightful scene of misery and death, continual slaughter, privation, and cruelty. Men, women, and children crowded around us, bewailing our departure, moving along with us in one great mass for some miles.

We passed the Escurial, that celebrated palace, built by Charles V, where his bones and those of so many kings of Spain were deposited with regal pomp. The great passeth away in his greatness, and a bit of a churchyard fits everybody!

Chapter Seventeen
Retreat!

Many peasants lay dead by the roadside, murdered, but by whom we did not know, and I doubt if any one cared, for death was so familiar in all shapes at that time. We crossed the Guadarama mountains, and a splendid sight it was to see so grand an army winding its way zig-zag up that long pass, as far as the eye could see from the top step, in the far distance. The old trade was going on, killing and slaying, and capturing our daily bread. When we got on to the plains on the other side, and crossed the Tormes, we expected some rest, a bit of sleep, and fetter rations, or some improvement in the foraging department, but things got worse and worse. I had been feasting the last few days on some bullock's liver without salt, and hard biscuit, abominable feeding until people come to know what hunger really is. We got near to Salamanca, and bivouacked in a cork wood. The oak trees too were large and numerous, and the acorns ripe and dropping from the branches. We were gathering, and roasting, and eating them all day, for the Commissary failed in issuing our common ration of biscuit. He served out instead a quarter pound of raw wheat to each man; this we pounded on a stone, and threw into the camp kettle with our beef, which thickened the soup! There was a little bit of growling now and then, much laughing and joking, but no complaint. Queer music it was to see and hear an army sitting on the sod, each man with two big stones grinding his dinner, but everything was sweet that came out of a camp kettle. It must be remembered that the British army had no tents, it was all bivouacking, *i.e.* lying out on the sod in all weather, like any other wild beasts, and always up and armed ready for anything one hour before daylight, and never dismissed until we could see a white horse a mile distant. This was always a very long hour, just unrolled from one's blanket to stand shivering in the early chill of a drizzly morning.

We had to be always ready for a move, or a march, or a change of ground, or a fight, as the bugle sounded. Always on the *"qui vive,"* night and day, and much need too, for we expected the army of France to be upon us at any moment. I bought a pony "on tick" just now, *i.e.* to be paid for by instalments as we might get our pay. This was the practice, and the price I paid was eighty dollars, being glad of anything to get my feet off the ground, I was so much knocked up. As for forage, my *caballo* was not entitled to forage, or anything but what he could pick up for himself. He would eat acorns like a pig, and lie down by the camp fire like a Christian at night. 'Yonder they come', is echoed by a hundred voices. The bugles sound, and the old word runs along, 'Fall in'.

The French now are seen in dense dark columns, crossing the Tormes by the fords. The train of artillery miles long, cavalry in front and on the flanks—all move on quietly towards us for a while, when they bring up their right shoulders and sweep along the base of the Aripiles out of our sight, but right under the eye of Wellington and his guns. From this point he offers to deliver battle to the French Marshal, but that crafty General will not accept the challenge. He had made an effort to get us into his net by a combination of movements, but would not fight. It is a great thing to fight an important battle against such a General as Wellington, and such troops as the British, and to win. But Soult might have been excused, if he thought twice before putting the life and fame of so many thousands upon the event of a day, for here, on this very ground, three months before, General Marmont was beaten, and his army nearly destroyed. Wellington now courted a battle on the Aripiles, or on the Tormes. He opened a cannonade, did all he could to invite them on, but no go, they declined to quarrel.

My regiment was formed in quarter-distance column on the breast of the hill ready for action, all the French on the other side out of our sight. Anxious as we were to get a peep at those ugly customers, we could not see one of them. An aide-de-camp came riding down the hill now, and asked our Colonel if he had a mounted officer.

'Yes, I believe there is one.'

'Please send him up to the crest of the hill there, where the Duke is with his staff, and let him report himself to the Quartermaster-General.'

'Always in luck,' said a few of my comrades, as I jumped on my dirty white steed.

'Yes,' I said, 'but there is bad as well as good luck at one's heels everywhere.'

'Never mind, come down and tell us, if we are going to fight today, for it is getting late.'

When I got up and swept my eye over the plain below, what a grand spectacle! The massive dark columns of the whole French army standing at ease or with arms piled; dragoons alongside their horses, and the guns limbered up, our artillery pounding at them without provoking a return shot. I saw they were beginning to move, so asked for my orders at once.

'Go off,' he said, 'as fast as you can to Algiho, and order the baggage of the 2nd Division to push on to Ciudad Rodrigo.'

'I don't know the way, sir. How am I to find the place? Nor do I know the distance.'

'Right in that direction,' he said, pointing with his glass, 'and the first village you come to ask for a guide: now be off, quick.'

I could now see that instead of a fight we were likely to continue our retreat; so I jogged on to the first village to get my guide. The town was empty and pillaged, inhabitants all gone, night was on me, I got bewildered, but rode on in the direction I was told as well as I could remember. As the dark clouds left the bright moon clear, I got a glimpse now and then of the skeletons of man and horse lying where they fell in the great battle of July, looking grim and ghastly.

How soon one loses his way if he shuts his eyes for a hundred yards! I ought not to have been here at all, the first hours of darkness put me all astray, and so I wandered on, not knowing where I was or where I was going, until I saw in the distance a corps of cavalry coming towards me. There was no cover on the plain where I could hide. My pony was white so I had no chance of escape; I could not evade the enemy. To France I must go a prisoner of war, and no mistake, if they thought me worth catching for the pony. As to my pockets, they were empty. I had not a dollar and was altogether nothing of a prize. I kept edging off on the flank, when I heard a loud English laugh. Oh, what a relief, how cheering—a regiment of our own cavalry!

'Where are you going?' I said.

'Up to the army. Where are you bound for?'

'Can hardly tell; to look after baggage in some forest, perhaps ten leagues off. You'll find the army in retreat from the Aripiles—good night.'

I went on my lonely way until I fell in with a Portuguese regiment in bivouac, close to a large town. I asked the name. 'Salamanca, *senor.*' Prodigious, entirely out of my line of march. However, I thought I might be still in luck, for our kind and generous paymaster I knew was here, and having been to see him a week before, I remembered his quarters and made my way there in the middle of the night, made a thundering noise at his door with a big stone. He popped his nightcap out of the window in alarm, with *'que quiera vmd?'*

'Oh, never mind talking Spanish to me, dear *Senor Pagadore*, let me in, for I'm half dead and my pony ditto.'

Kind, amiable, good fellow, he came down directly, in amazement to find me so far away out of my place. I soon told him all. The pony was brought into the house and got some provender.

'And now' he said, 'go off to the *alcalde* and get a guide for tomorrow, while I am getting your dinner, tea, and supper ready, for you look starved.'

There was a great stir in the city, of course, and the chief office of police open all the night. I asked for a guide in the name of Wellington.

The chief man present, an uncouth-looking savage, said 'Take that fellow beside you,' pointing to a *pizanno* in the dirty crowd.

'I don't know the way, senor.'

'Take him away,' he said, 'he's a *ladrone,* and knows the country well.'

So I drew my sword, and walked him off to the paymaster's, and locked him up for the rest of the night. I had a most excellent feed, and had my haversack stored for the march next day. I lay down for three hours' sleep, my very kind friend keeping watch to have me up in time, and not letting me go without a few dollars in my pocket. I was away early with my guide, who was very loquacious and very hungry, as he said, and I believed him, but declined allowing him to go home just for ten minutes, to *comer* (to eat). I gave him a piece of bread and beef out of my wallet, and we became great friends until we arrived at the next village, when he gave me the slip. He doubled round a corner with an '*Adios, senor*', and I saw no more of him!

I got another vagabond guide here, a piece of pork, four potatoes, and two loaves of bread, and took my journey onwards without the slightest knowledge of where I was going. It appeared that this fellow was taking me to his own native village, and when we got there he bolted off like a shot, and left me on the road. On foot I might have kept him beside me, but on horseback I had no chance. So it is between cavalry and infantry; vain and fruitless to match the sabre with the musket, to send the charging horsemen against the foot-soldier. I have seen the squadrons cheering on loudly, and at full speed closing on the infantry squares, when they were instantly scorched and scattered by the peal of musketry. As the smoke cleared, the British bayonets glittered and the regiment came forth unscathed as from a furnace.

I rode on a few leagues farther in a mysterious jumble of thought about responsibility, and the wild orders I had received. I met a multitude of the peasantry, men, women and children, all laden with their little household goods and traps, the matrons marching erect with babies in little cork baskets balanced on their heads.

'Where are you all going?' I said.

'O, *senor*, come back with us to Salamanca. The French are behind us, our town pillaged, the English all killed, and you will be a prisoner.'

Poor people, I was sorry for them, but thought I would not give up my wild-goose chase upon this report, and rode on. I soon met another batch with the same tale, and turned back with them, being satisfied that I really was on very dangerous ground. As it happened I met with my old regiment crossing my path, and joyfully did I fall into my old place, after making a full report of my journey to the good Colonel Fenwick. My haversack was soon lightened by a few of my hungry comrades, but still I held on to the pork and potatoes with a loaf of bread in reserve!

The whole British army was now in full retreat. The rains had set in, the weather had become dreadful, and we were sorely pressed by the enemy; all dreary and desolate, marching and fighting all day, tired and hungry but not desponding. My regiment being in its turn one day on the rear guard, we halted by the edge of an oak wood to cook, and I rode over to a cottage a little way off very wet. I asked the *patrona*, a poor old woman, to make up a good fire, and give me a little pot to cook my dinner, which being done *con amore*, I then pulled off my boots and socks, and put them to the fire.

'And your coat, *senor*', said the good woman.

I made room for that too, put the piece of pork and the potatoes in the one pot, and sat there in great luxury. Everything was going on as nice as in a restaurant and getting so dry. My landlady was heaping on sticks and the pot boiling, when she came bustling in, greatly alarmed, with '*O, senor, los Franceses—los Franceses!*' I heard a distant shot and looked out. Sure enough, and to my horror, there was a French cavalry corps feeling their way up to the wood, where the smoke of our fires told them a tale. A few more stray shots; I looked out. The bugle sounded; there were men falling in after upsetting their half-cooked rations and shoving the beef part into I their haversacks; all hurry-scurry and long shots at the cavalry. I got on my toggery, pretty well dried, and bolted out of the cabin just in time to fall in while my corps was forming square against those bold dragoons. They were very plucky, but great spoons to match themselves against a regiment of infantry without support. We emptied some of their saddles, when they retired to re-form, and wait for their advance-guard of foot-soldiers coming up. In the meantime we got into the wood and continued our course. I lamented all the day for the loss of my dinner, which I carried so far and left at last to be devoured by a Frenchman. How the men did swear at them!

'If the vagabonds had come on after dinner, sure they'd

be welcome, but just as our pots were on the boil—O, bad luck to them, and may they never see home!'

The enemy followed, and pressed us hard until night, when they bivouacked. We did the same, after a good start in advance. It rained hard, and the ground was in one great swamp. We had no baggage, it being all in front, as is usual in retreat. I got up into a cork tree, amongst the thick branches, and balanced myself there until we moved on, about four o'clock in the morning. This was a hard day upon the men, from the heavy rains. Many fell out, some sick, others disabled and footsore. Hundreds broke down, overcome by the great weight they had to carry, in addition to the wet clothes on the back—viz. a knapsack, heavy old flint firelock, sixty rounds of ball cartridge, haversack with sometimes three days' rations, wooden canteen, bayonet, greatcoat, and blanket—half-choked with a stiff leather girdle about the throat, and as many cross buff belts as would harness a donkey. It was wonderful how they moved along, and more surprising that they were not all left on the line of march. As it was, the French were picking them up in scores as they dotted the cheerless route.

We gained our bivouac at a late hour, made our fires, and prepared for supper—a hard biscuit and the remnant of a carrion ration of beef, no rum. We finished the little we had by the way. Our Commissary (Brook) came up now with the mules and stores, pitched his tent beside us, and looked so comfortable, that three of us cast lots as to who would go on a sort of forlorn hope and ask or beg of him to give us a ration of rum to keep in life till morning. I braced up all my courage, went forth, and demanded an audience.

'Hard times, Brook, three of us here beside you, famished. Will you give us a drop of rum?'

'And then,' he said, 'I will have the whole camp on the

top of me, and my supply short already.'

'Honour bright,' I said, 'close as a pill-box.'

He called one of his people and told him to fill my flask. My flask happened, luckily for me, to be my wooden canteen, which held about three pints, and the generous muleteer filled it up to the brim, and away I went joyful. Little as this trifle may appear, it was more than gold could purchase, and raised our barometer amazingly. Our luck was not yet over, the moon came peering through clouds of rain, when a herd of innocent, friendly swine wandered in amongst the men. This was tempting beyond all endurance. Thousands of hungry soldiers by fires blazing bright, hundreds of well-fed pigs at the very point of the bayonet, the camp already yielding in anticipation a perfume of pork chops, who could let these wanderers of the dark forest pass away without further acquaintance? It would not be etiquette; but now, against all military discipline, a hundred shots were fired almost simultaneously. The mudlarks were knocked over right and left. The bivouac was all in alarm, the drums beat to arms, bugles sounded the assembly, the men groped their way to their alarm-posts, every one supposing that the enemy were upon us (barring the pig-shooters). The general officers kicked up a frightful dust about this unaccountable midnight row. Nobody did it, it was all the fault of intruders. However, before morning there was a savoury smell of roast pork about our fires, and no further inquiry. I found a small joint beside me, left there by the fairies, not over nicely dressed, the bristles like porcupine quills, but well fed.

The Duke made a great fuss about all this insubordination. But it is to be remembered that the line of march from Salamanca was through a flooded and flat clay country, that the troops, ankle-deep in mire, mid-leg in water, had lost their shoes; and with strained sinews had heavily made their way upon two rations only in five days, feeding on acorns, when Wellington supposed that the Commissaries were supplying the army with their usual rations.

The great Commander, in whom we had the firmest reliance, was unrivalled in skill, vigour, and genius, but could not see at once into the wants and necessities of 70,000 men. The pursuing enemy captured much of our stores and baggage, and our loss of seasoned British soldiers on this retreat, in killed and wounded, and prisoners, according to the returns, came up to 8,000 men. War tries the strength of military framework and hunger will not resist a pork-chop fried on the top of a ramrod.

'The pigs,' men said, 'had no right poaching on our grounds, and we had a right to our ration of acorns.'

When we came to rivers, there was no halting or hesitation. The men walked in and over, as if on parade; when pretty deep, they linked together to break the stream. In fording the Duero, near Toro, we found it so deep and rapid, that the men slung their ammunition on the back of their necks to keep it dry. Our baggage being in advance, it made one wince to think of the chance of the poor little donkeys crossing this gulf with all our treasure on their back, and it was many a long day before we heard the fate of our respective quadrupeds. Many were lost with their precious load, and there was no compensation.

A multitude of soldiers' wives stuck to the army like bricks. Averse to all military discipline, they impeded our progress at times very much, particularly in this retreat. They became the subject of a general order for their own special guidance. They were under no control, and were first mounted up and away in advance, blocking up narrow passages, and checking the advance of the army with their donkeys, after repeated orders to follow in rear of their respective corps, or their donkeys would be shot.

'I'd like to see the man that wud shoot my donkey says Mrs. Biddy Flyn, 'faith I'll be too early away for any of 'em to catch me. Will you come wid me, girls?'

'Aye, indeed, every one of us,' and away they all started at early dawn, cracking their jokes about division orders, Wellington, commanding officers, and their next bivouac.

Mrs. Skiddy led the way on her celebrated donkey called the 'Queen of Spain'. She was a squat little Irishwoman, and broad as a big turtle.

'Dhrive on, girls, and we'll bate them to the end ov this day, at any rate,' says Mother Skiddy.

'An' the morrow, too,' says Mrs. Flyn.

'An' the day after,' cried Betty Wheel, and then a chorus of laughter by the whole brigade (those three industrious women will be remembered by any old 34th man still alive).

Alas! the Provost-Marshal was in advance—a man in authority, and a terror to all evil-doers. In his department the *Habeas Corpus* Act was suspended throughout the war, and he was waiting here in a narrow turn of the road for the ladies with an advance guard, all loaded. He gave orders to fire at once on the donkeys, killing and wounding two or three, *pour exemple.* There was a wild, fierce, and furious yell struck up at once, with more weeping and lamentation than one generally hears at an Irish funeral, with sundry prayers for the vagabond that murdered the lives of these poor, darling, innocent crathers! As we came up, the cries of distress echoed in the hollow trunks of the old cork trees.

It was 'Oh, bad luck to his ugly face—the spy of our camp—may he nivver see home till the vultures pick his eyes out, the born varmint,' and so on.

They gathered up what they could carry, and marched on along with the troops, crying and lamenting their bitter fate, with not a dry rag on their backs.

It was wonderful what they endured; but, in spite of all this warning, Mother Skiddy was foremost on the line of march next morning, as she said, 'We must risk something to be in before the men, to have the fire an' a dhrop of tay ready for the poor crathers after their load an' their labour. An' sure if I went in the rare, the French, bad luck to them, wud pick me up, me an' my donkey, and then Dan would be lost entirely.'

She was a devoted soldier's wife, and a right good one, an excellent forager, and never failed to have something for Dan when we were all starving. Dan Skiddy was not much bigger than his wife—short and stumpy, but with great bone and pluck, and of good character. I carried his firelock for him at times many a mile, when he was ready to drop, as he said, with rheumatiz pains.

Our long and weary wet march of seventeen days came to an end at last. During all the time I don't think I was perfectly dry for twenty-four hours. Our Brigadier, General Wilson, an old man with a grey head, who rode a blind horse, was always very plucky in showing the men how to cross a stream. When they hesitated on its brink, he would dismount, walk in with the greatest nonchalance, and remount with his boots full of water. But this practice did not agree with his years or constitution, 'and he died'.

The French did not get fat on our trail. Heaps of heavy baggage and broken-down soldiers fell to their lot, but little to eat. Our good paymaster, J--, offered a poor peasant one day a doubloon (sixteen dollars) for a loaf of bread.

He said, '*Senor*, I can't eat your gold; I am starving myself' —so hard were we pressed at times for food. But these little incidents in a campaign were soon forgotten, and never entered into the columns of an English newspaper.

We got into the mountains bordering on Portugal, and the army was soon distributed amongst the towns and villages in Estremadura, very celebrated for fever and ague. The little village of Caza-don-Comez sufficed to give covering to my regiment; bad as it was, we rejoiced at the change. I lodged with a very poor peasant in a very humble dwelling. He herded goats all day on the hills, was dressed in sheep-skins, and returned at night to the family meal, which he always prepared himself. It never varied; a loaf of brown bread sliced into a wooden bowl, some olive-oil poured over it, then some hot water, and mixed up. He and his wife and children sat round with their spoons and kept time till the dish was cleared out. None of the party ever spoke a word until the evening meal was finished. In this humble way they lived and seemed contented. In their simplicity and poverty there was a courteous hospitality, such as never sitting down without asking me to partake of their supper. I had a little sort of a bed in a recess in the kitchen, near the fire, where we all sat of an evening by the light of some sticks, a very taciturn party. I was hardly domiciled here when I was taken ill of a fever, accompanied by total prostration of strength and physical power. I don't remember how long I lay in the corner. The regimental surgeon came daily to see if I was dead or alive. He had nothing to give me but a kind and encouraging word. Men died here by the score for want of care and medical comforts.

Poor Robert S— and I were very great friends, but he had nothing but his carving tools, blue pill and salts, and his good name, which carried him through an honourable life with success. I met him accidentally long afterwards in India in a *choultry* by the way side, and years after I returned from the Burmese war we were stationed in the same beautiful cantonment at Bangalore.

We got a little of our back pay on account at this time, and I was able to provide some tea, sugar, and bread for myself—all that I cared for. I got some of the goats' milk for my tea, which I considered a perfect luxury. The rough edge was wearing off the winter, brighter days shining through dark clouds. Change of quarters and returning health cheered me up a bit when I thought I was left here forlorn to die in a hovel, but I was never forsaken. There was a bright star above to guide and protect even the thoughtless and unworthy, and so far strength of frame and energy of mind had borne me scatheless and uninjured through scenes of fatigue, and danger, and blood, and death. I had been pining after home in my long illness, but as health came gradually rolling back, and rousing me up, I soon forgot the feeling.

I had sold my pony to pay for himself, and was again on my pins, a foot-soldier. There never was any objection to an officer keeping a horse and riding on the line of march, but he got no forage beyond the usual allowance—that is, two Subs were allowed forage for one baggage animal. When we came to a scrimmage on the line of march at any time, we quickly dismounted and sent our steeds to the rear. If they were killed in action we bore the loss, besides having a better chance of being killed also.

My regiment moved to another little village, just able to hold us all, and no more. So we had it all to ourselves and a pretty, cheerful little place it was. The people were poor, but very simple, honest, and kind in their way.

We got clear away from the Spanish army for a time. They were incapable of any dexterous movement. No master spirit was amongst them, and they continually worried our great chief with their apathy, intrigue, and dogged habits of indolence, faction, and violence. Their insolence and ferocity at Salamanca were in famous. One instance is well known: a horse, led by an English soldier, being frightened, backed against a Spanish officer, commanding at a gate. He caused the soldier to be dragged into his guard-house, and there destroyed him in cold blood with bayonet wounds! There was nothing for it but counter-violence.

Another Spanish officer wantonly stabbed at a rifleman, who shot him at once. A British volunteer slew a Spanish officer at the head of his own regiment in a sword fight, the troops of both nations looking on; but here there was nothing dishonourable.

Our kind, good, and amiable soldier-chief, General Sir Rowland Hill, had a little pack of hounds sent out from England at this period to afford some field sport to his division. There was no lack of the sly fox; plenty of red-coats in the field, and good horsemen too. Crossing a plain one day in full chase, Reynard disappeared all at once. The foremost horseman had but just time to pull up at the edge of a rocky precipice, when they discovered poor Reynard and nine of the hounds below, all dead!

The General's headquarters were at Coria, about two leagues from us. He encouraged any amusement likely to afford pleasure to his officers, and now he patronised an amateur theatre, which was very well got up. We had amongst so many regiments capital actors, scene-painters, and really a first-rate company. The delicate-looking, pale-faced, slim Ensigns distinguished themselves in petticoats, and right well they played their parts. All we wanted was an audience! We had some very handsome Spanish *senoras*, who looked on and laughed through their bright eyes, but understood nothing. There was one fair and beautiful Englishwoman always present, joyous and happy, a charming representative of those bright stars of Albion, whose presence was always cheering amongst so many red-coats, the only lady at headquarters, wife of Colonel C—, Hill's first aide-de-camp, who afterwards fell at Waterloo.

After the play we all went in our stage dresses to the General's supper table, where we did enjoy ourselves to the full, a singular-looking group of painted actors and actresses. I can now see his good, honest, benevolent face shining with delight at the head of his table, enjoying the scene and the songs that went round until a late hour. He was the man who never could say an ill word to anyone; the Duke's favourite and most successful General. His sobriquet was 'Farmer Hill', while another was called Tiger C--, and so on. Every General, as well as regiment, had a nick-name. But there was a mutual confidence that could not be shaken between the parties, and they, one and all, had the firmest reliance on Wellington. He never came near us without a cheer from the men that made the woods ring. When he appeared, the men would say, 'There he comes with his long nose, boys; you may fix your flints'.

My Captain, Egerton, or, as the girls called him, '*Senor quatro-ojos*', or four eyes, as he wore spectacles, was a fine specimen of a Cheshire gentleman and a brave soldier. He had gone on General Hill's staff as chief aide-de-camp, and was always my friend, until he finished off his campaign, a general officer on his native ground.

1813. We were very busy with parades and drills and field-days, and some little horse racing in April. Large reinforcements of cavalry and infantry arrived from England, and the whole British army was being reorganised by the great chief for the coming struggle. Our ranks were filled up by officers and men, all 'Johnnie Newcomes' of course, but were soon drilled into a new form of discipline, which rather astonished some of their backs. They were men, chiefly volunteers from the Militia, who seemed to have had a little too much of their own way. But that was soon drilled out of them, and they were taught that the first duty of a soldier is 'to obey orders'. Amongst the officers, a nice-looking lad named Phillips, about seventeen, with June roses on his cheeks, stuck to me, and we ran in couples very happy during his brief campaign, which ended on the battlefield in less than four months. I grieved after this lad very much, so young, so brave, so full of life and joy.

Since we finished off the retreat from Burgos and Madrid there was great mortality amongst the troops, fever and ague prevailing. I caught both and suffered severely. There was no cure. All the charms the doctors got from the medical department at home was some rotten old bark intended to be mixed with some country wine, to dose the soldiers. Some fusty sawdust would have had the same effect! Lives were held cheap, but they cost money, nobody cared: 'things will last my time', and the national debt will probably last a while longer!

Chapter Eighteen
Farewell Portugal

On the 1st of May Wellington mounted his gallant steed, took a last look across the hills, and saying, 'Farewell, Portugal!' headed his grand army to do or die in this campaign.

Three of us young fellows clubbed up a little mess. I was the best provided of the party with everything, as my baggage got safe over the retreat. I bought another donkey on the strength of all Subs being allowed forage for one animal. Our kind and generous paymaster made me a present of a very pretty Spanish jennet, and now I was all right and ready for the road, barring the ague, which left me prostrate every second day. The cold shivering fit first came on, nothing would warm me, then after a few hours the hot or burning fever fit succeeded, with a splitting headache that nearly drove me crazy. The next day I was quite well and fit for anything.

We now broke up from our cantonments, and the very first day was my ague day, and somehow doubly severe. I suffered dreadfully. Unable to keep my saddle, I tied my horse to a tree, lay down beside him until the last fit passed away, and then followed my corps to the camping ground. I was sometimes detained until long after dark, when my messmates were sure to have something for me along with the tea, always a stand-by and a luxury.

We commenced this campaign with tents for officers and men. The mules that formerly carried the camp kettles now carried the tents. The old large iron cooking-kettles were put *hors-de-combat*, and replaced by smaller tin kettles which were carried by the men in addition to their usual load. Captains had a mule allowed to carry a tent (and some company books, etc.) for himself and his Subs.

I had the fortune, good or bad, to be once more in the company of 'Bloody Mick' of former days. He had the politeness to say at the start that I might occupy a corner of his tent at night. I knew very well I had as much right there as himself, but the invitation was not so hospitable as to induce me to sleep in the same house with my gallant Captain. I preferred the outside, and slept under a tree on the sod for two months, when I was transferred to the Light Company, one of the Subs thereof being taken prisoner in a scrimmage with the French.

My Captain (Fancourt) was a first-rate fellow, a fine and gallant soldier, always generous, hospitable, and kind. I never left him afterwards. He was the best dressed man in the army, very fond of horses, and always well mounted.

Joking one day with our Commissary Barlow, he said, 'I wish you would give me a little barley for my horse, I am very hard run over for a feed.'

'Do you see that sack-full there? It contains rations for three mules for ten days; if you will carry it to your quarters on your back you may have it—mind, no help.'

Fancourt peeled off his red coat, made one great effort, got under the sack and carried it out of the store, through the town, to his quarters amidst hurrahs and 'Well done, old fellow, you have done the Commissary'. He dropped his burden at his stable door with a face as red as a peony with laughter and exertion! He would have shared his rations with his horse at any time if hard pressed. Commissary Barlow never made him a similar offer, although they were ever good friends.

The weather was very fine and very dry. It was rather agreeable sleeping under the trees at night although the dews were heavy. To keep dry I generally cut a bundle of fine branches to lie on, rolled myself in my blanket, put my saddle under my head, tied my bonny black jennet to a tree, gave him the length of his tether to feed, and went to sleep myself until the bugle sounded before dawn, when I had the night dew shaken out of my blanket, placed it as usual under my saddle and marched away. The men were generally cheerful and full of mirth for the first few leagues, when they began to labour along in silence until they reached the next lodging-ground to shake off their load for the night.

Wellington led on his brave army with confidence to a succession of victories. We crossed the Douro and the Ebro in our line of march, the army divided into many columns, and were not long in scenting out the enemy. I went on the Burgos road with General Hill. His orders were, I believe, to fight there or take the fortress. It cost us 2,000 the last visit, and here we fully expected another slaughter, but King Joseph Bonaparte had not the masterspirit of Soult, whom he disliked.

As we advanced, he retreated from Burgos. The castle had been prepared for destruction, and I was not sorry at being awoke one night out of my tired slumbers on the green sod by an awful explosion, like an earthquake. I drew myself up, half-asleep, into a sitting posture and said, 'Thank God! there goes Burgos,' and lay down again to finish my slumbers. But with the castle 300 souls were blown into eternity! At the moment I cared little for that; such is war! From hurry or neglect, the mine exploded before its time, several streets were laid in ruins, thousands of shells ignited and exploded and rolled about with destructive power. And so this great impediment in our way was finally removed, just as we could have wished, except the terrible death of 300 of our enemies. In war, nothing so bad as failure or defeat, and this must have damped the King's courage a bit. His brother, the great Napoleon, they say, used to tell him that if he would command, he must give himself up entirely to business, labouring day and night: just the thing he never was cut out for, as will be found recorded in his history. Indeed, his cognomen was '*Roi de Bouteille*'. He had a fine command, a great and brilliant army, an obedient army; but that soul of armies, the mind of a great com-mander, was wanting. It was all on our side, in Wellington's knowledge-box! and nothing now retarded his progress. With an eagle's sweep he poured his columns through all the deep narrow valleys and rugged defiles, gullies, ravines, and passes, amongst the rocks. Nothing even retarded the march of the artillery: where horses could not go nor draw, the soldiers did their work; and when the wheels could not roll, guns were let down or lifted up with ropes. Bravely did our rough veteran infantry work their way for six days, with unceasing toil, through those wild and beautiful regions.

Our army, swelling in numbers, came rushing in from hill and vale and valley, like roaring streams from every defile, foaming into the basin of Vittoria. When the King was conjecturing about the quickest way to put the English army *hors-de-combat*, and at what hour he might consistently partake of the banquet he had ordered in Vittoria, Wellington was making his arrangements to cook him before sunset. The 20th of June was my ague day. I was wearied and worn with this horrid complaint persecuting me every second day for the last two months, but I was not singular. However, I stuck to my trade and resisted being left in hospital at any of the depots formed in our rear—perfectly well today, tomorrow in torture, dejected and cast down. I lay under a tree, seeing my comrades pass away over the plain. Night came on, I rose like one from the dead and followed in their wake. My chums had some tea ready for me, with something in the frying-pan, when I got into camp.

We knew little or nothing of what was to come off

the following day, except from our men, who were fixing their flints, chaffing and talking of the 'frog eaters' who could not be far off. They said they 'nosed them from their backie and inions!' I declined the tent accommodation, and slept soundly on the sod. We were all under arms right early in the morning, the rolls were called, all present, and nobody afraid! It was a bright, warm, and beautiful day —the longest day—and a long day's work was before us, before the sun was to set on so many of the brave. We had scarcely advanced a league across the plain when we heard the riflemen on our left beginning the work of the morning; cheers through the ranks, many jokes and quaint sayings. There was great hilarity, buoyant spirit and cheerfulness, a determined resolve to fight to the front, and never say die. When the British soldier is let loose in the field with all his steam up, the difficulty is to keep him in check, to stop his onward rapidity. When he sees the enemy in his front, he fights for his Queen, fights for Old England, fights for victory, and always wins. The British soldier is a queer sort of biped, fierce in battle, full of a child's simplicity and kindness when over. He will tear the shirt off his back to bind up the bleeding wounds of his fallen foe, carry him away on his back to some quiet spot for medical care, lay him gently down, and divide with him the contents of his flask.

Chapter Nineteen
The Battle of Vittoria

Twenty soldiers may give a descriptive account of a battle, all different, yet all correct. It is impossible for one man to see the entire of a battlefield ten or fifteen miles in extent, even on the swiftest horse. One intelligent, active mind can gather in a great deal from personal observation, and collect from other sources much information and truth, and unless a truthful narrative is recorded in a journal like this, it is not worth the printer's ink. There was no man of our day could give a more thrilling descriptive account of a battlefield than the brave and gallant veteran Sir W. Napier.

The river Zadora ran through the whole line of the battleground for many miles, and was spanned by seven bridges. It was about ten o'clock before we (2nd Division) got into action. General Hill had 20,000 men, and moved them on the left of the French position, when we began with a sharp skirmish, and renewed the old quarrel. We soon began to warm to the old work, and matters looked serious. We won a hill on which the enemy were strongly posted, but at a severe loss. The Hon. Colonel Cadogan, commanding the 71st Regiment, was killed here, with many other valuable officers.

We were gaining ground along the side of the mountain, when we met with a biting fire, and the battle here remained stationary for some time, until our General sent us more aid. Then, passing the Zadora, we won the village of Subijana-de-Alava, in front of General Gazan, and maintained our ground in spite of all opposition.

There was a good deal of fighting in the churchyard, and some open graves were soon filled up with double numbers; indeed, churches and churchyards were always a favourable resort for this peculiar amusement. They were places of strength, and contended for accordingly; and here our battle raged with more violence and contention. We had possession—nine-tenths of the law in battle—but, hardly pressed front and flank, I thought we had killed more of our French neighbours here than was needful; but as they cared little for life in their excitement, they would be killed. As Colonel Brown said, 'If you don't kill them, boys, they'll kill you; fire away.'

There were three great battles going on. The curling smoke in the far away distance and booming of guns showed that our comrades were deeply engaged with all the destructive power at their disposal. Our wretched old flint firelocks would not burn powder at times until the soldier took from the pocket in his pouch a triangle screw, to knock life into his old flint, and then clear the touch-hole with a long brass picker that hung from his belt. Many a fellow was killed while performing this operation. But the French had no better fighting tools than ourselves, so in this respect we were not unequally matched. However, the red-coats got impatient and excited to be at them with the bayonet, and when the word was delivered 'Prepare to charge', the very hills echoed back the mighty cheer of thousands with an overwhelming terror, for the charge was irresistible.

Upon all favourable occasions our men were let loose in this way to complete a victory. Our opponents never liked the steel, it was so indigestible, and at this part of the play the *En avant* was never heard, but rather *Sauve qui peut*.

It was now about one o'clock. The whole line of the battle-field was in a blaze—guns, mortars, cavalry, and infantry displaying double exertion and courage to win the day. Seventy thousand brave men, not fearing death nor danger, on each side were contending for a kingdom that must be lost or won this day. Yes, this 21st day of June 1813 must decide the fate of Spain.

Morillo's Spaniards displayed unusual courage, and fought well, himself wounded. But Longa would not move his troops when they were required at a very critical moment, just like the old mule. Our troops plunged into the village of Arinez amidst a heavy fire of musketry and artillery. This was an important post. Fresh French troops came pouring down to the bloody work. The smoke, dust, and clamour, the flashing of firearms, the shouts and cries of the combatants, mixed with the thundering of the guns, were terrible. The continuous cries, of the wounded for water were piteous, while the horses, distracted and torn with cannon-shot, were hobbling about in painful torture, some with broken legs, and others dragging their entrails after them in mad career. It was indeed a sickening sight I never wished to see again, but my heart and eyes were since in time to be tortured with more dreadful scenes. As we gained this village and advanced, many guns were captured. It was a country of high corn, vineyards, wood and plain, ditches, villages, hamlets, and the river winding right away down to the Ebro. We had now fought over about six miles of country, yet the French were not quelled nor beaten. General Reille maintained his post on their last high ground, and made his muskets flash like lightning, while fourscore pieces of artillery, nearly all fired together, made a furious uproar that shook the earth, and ground our men to pulp before they had time to make the dash. Amidst the fire and smoke, the dark figures of the French artillery were seen bounding about, and serving their guns with frantic energy. This terrible cannonade and fire of small-arms checked our troops until the 4th Division came up; they needed no introduction to General Reille. With one long loud cheer, an electric shock to Frenchmen's nerves, this important position was won at a rush.

In other places the battle was waged with fury and great energy on both sides. The day was not yet won; it was the longest, and in every respect the most bloody day that many of us had ever seen, but I had little time to think about it.

A Spanish *pisanno* told Lord Wellington that one of the bridges was undefended, and offered to lead any troops to it. A brigade was immediately sent forward, and while passing over it at the double, the poor fellow at their head was killed by a cannon-shot.

About six o'clock the whole of the French army was beaten back to their last defence, about a mile from Vittoria. Behind them was the plain, and beyond the city. Thousands of non-combatants, carriages, men, women, and children belonging to the host of the great army, were crowded together in wild terror. Our cannon-shot went booming over their heads, which threw them into a convulsive movement of distress. They swarmed together, swerved, looked about for safety; but there was no hope now for the multitude or the army. They lost the day. It was now the wreck of a nation—of a great army in all its power and pride and glory, led by a King and the most efficient and accomplished Generals of an Emperor. Twelve hours ago the balance of military power on the plains of 'Old Castile' was about equal; but there was a confiding reliance throughout our ranks in the skill of our great chief that never was shaken, and defeat was never named. Yet we did, if truth must be told, get rather a severe kick in one month after this by these very well-beaten Frenchmen, or by some of their relations or friends.

The British army closely pursued the flying and shattered columns of the French, now broken and dispersed, until night stopped the chase. Never was there a more complete victory, and, as General Gazan said, 'They lost all their equipages, all their guns, all their treasure, all their stores, all their papers—so that no man could prove how much pay was due to him.'

Generals and subordinate officers were reduced to the clothes on their backs, and most of them barefooted. The trophies were very numerous. Marshal Jourdan's baton, a stand of colours, 140 brass cannon, all their stores, carriages, and ammunition, their treasure, and prisoners too many to enable us to pay attention to their wants and safety. They lost 6,000 men. Our loss was nearly equal, 5,176; of these, according to returns, 1,049 were Portuguese, and 553 were Spaniards, our loss being more than double that of our two friendly powers. In fact, the red-coats were always expected to do the real fighting business. British troops are the soldiers of the battle.

Chapter Twenty
Pursuit

The spoil was very great; it may be said that the fighting men were marching and fighting upon gold and silver,' without helping themselves. Five million dollars, abandoned by the French and left upon the ground, were picked up by non-combatants and camp followers. There were little barrels of doubloons and Napoleons in gold, for the picking up, but rather heavy to put into one's haversack. The chase was so swift, and the men so excited, that but a few just stumbled over this treasure, nor would any man be permitted to stop a moment if observed, yet a great many did fill their pockets and haversacks, and holsters with loose treasure just *en passant*, and kept on blazing away like fun. Not a dollar ever came to our treasury as prize money, which the Duke complained of; but, as for this, it was no great loss to us Subs, for we were always cheated of all but one-tenth of our share, and received that six years after the Peninsular war, and fourteen years after the first Burmese war. However, I only speak for myself. I know the time, and place, and amount I received, and the sum total did not come up to £20! My losses were more than five times as much.

But to continue our pursuit: the wreck of the army was in full retreat, their contest ended. The allies being now advancing on every point caused their confusion to increase, the guns were abandoned, the drivers rode off the horses at speed, the soldiers pressed wildly through a road half choked-up with the unfortunate refugees from the capital, and the vast number of vehicles which moved along with them in their flight. A scene of the most frightful disorder ensued. The sun now began to sink below the western hills, and the last rays of golden light fell upon a spectacle not easily described. Red columns of infantry were advancing steadily over the plain. The horse artillery were galloping to the front to open a fresh fire into the fugitives, the cavalry charging along the Camino Real; while the 2nd (Hill's) Division, which, overcoming every obstacle, had driven the enemy from its front, was extending along the heights and lower ground, on the right of the British army, its arms flashing brightly in the fading sunshine of this ever-memorable day. (Our arms now are brown: in former days they were bright and glittering in the sun or moonlight march.)

Never was a victory so complete, nor an army so very well thrashed and disorganised as this great French host. The bright and warm sun of a June morning rose on three united grand corps, all speaking the same language, perfect in every arm, admirably combined, and placed in a position of battle well selected and defended with batteries and breastworks, a river in their front, and all the chances of war in their favour. Night closed upon a pitiful and helpless, broken-down, dislocated, and shattered rabble, hurrying away from the fatal field of their defeat. The day was ours, but one could not help feeling deeply for the helpless multitude when our cannon-shot plunged amongst such a crowd of humanity trying to escape. Like the Scottish monarch at Flodden (just three hundred years ago, 1513), King Joseph remained to witness the ruin which his rashness wrought, but not to expiate his folly with his life. He effected his not very glorious retreat with difficulty. Our dragoons overtook and fired at his carriage, out of which he escaped by jumping, mounting a horse, and riding, harder than ever John Gilpin did, for life and liberty, guarded by a strong escort. He made Pampeluna that night without the value of a horn spoon of all his treasure.

I happened to be marching along in his track, and came upon his carriage upset in a ditch, and also seven waggons loaded with his personal baggage jammed up in a heap: the mules all gone; soldiers excitingly engaged, their muzzles black with powder from biting the cartridges, and perspiring like hunters, all busily employed stripping the carriage even of its lining in search of something portable in the shape of the image and superscription of Napoleon.

I never saw such handy fellows. So expert were they that the whole contents were laid before the public in about fifteen minutes for selection, or, as a Paddy of a Grenadier said, 'Come, boys, help yourselves wid anything yes like best, free gratis for nothing at all! The King soon made his will and left all you see behind him for our day's throuble. He's away to France, an' the de--l's luck to him! Who'll have a dhrink o' wine?'

And so they cracked their jokes at the expense of His Majesty. Another party were actively engaged unloading the waggons, pitching into the whole contents—trunks, boxes, great bundles of papers, letters private and confidential, charts, pictures of great value, which had been cut out of their frames, best French wines, brandy, beds and bedding, portable furniture, a whole library of books, everything in the cuisine department, camp equipage, and lots of grog corked and ready for this fatigue, party; with skins of Spanish wine, and a multiplication of other things which had belonged to this robber king, too tedious to be inserted in this bill of fare! I picked up hastily a big sack, a cold fowl, a few maps, and a flask of wine, the sum total of all the plunder I touched that day, and rode on.

Wellington went back to Vittoria about nine o'clock, still day-light, where all was panic and confusion. Every door was closed, every lattice darkened, the streets funereal and deserted, where two nights before all was brilliant and gay. The game took an unlucky turn for all Spaniards of the French party, many of whom went off with the retreating robbers. The loyalists now began to crow, and received Wellington with welcome cheers. During the progress of the battle, over three leagues of difficult country, the long summer's day was spent in an unremitting succession of laborious exertions to attain this great end. It was not generally a night of repose. There was a grand general auction in the camp of every brigade. The great variety of articles for sale was far beyond anything ever heard of, and if one was to attempt to enumerate them, would be beyond belief. How they were picked up so quickly by fighting men, who kept their fighting place, would astonish the reader. But when an army finds itself beaten and receives the word *sauve qui peut*, away they go, d—l take the hindmost, and as 'light marching order' is the swiftest retreat, they cast away everything as they run, arms, ammunition, firelocks, knapsack, and accumulation of plunder, which our men picked up in their advance. When they stumbled over a cask of dollars, in went the head with a punch from the butt-end of a firelock; the cask then rolled over, an inviting spread, and everyone helped himself and pushed on.

At this great night fair dollars were sold eight or nine for a guinea, or a Napoleon—too heavy to carry! In Spain the British army were paid in old English guineas and dollars. The 21st was my good day. I had no ague, but felt tired and excited after such a fight and a chase, for my horse was in the rear until the grand retreat began. It being now late, we halted for the night. I rode into a field of corn, so very high I could not be observed. Here I dismounted, sat down and ate my supper, provided by the cook of His Majesty or some of his people! I tied my gentle little horse to my leg, gave him a long tether, lay down upon my sack and fell asleep, *tout de suite*. Now and then 'Sancho' would get too far nibbling at the corn and give me chuck. I pulled him in by the rope close to my bed, and soon fell over again in dreams of peace and home. I was very early astir, and found my companion, cheval noir, lying beside me. He was a great pet and a handsome fellow. Saddled, mounted, and away to look for my regiment which was scattered about without any regularity in bivouac. But Freeman's bugle, so well known to every 34th man, soon brought us all together—no, not all, the prison of many a soul was broken up.

My servants were generally in great luck, having their legs and arms broken by musket-shot, and none of them killed outright except Tim Casey, and he was only kilt.

But he made a most horrible *whilalaloo* about it, crying out, 'Oh, murdher, I'm kilt entirely. I'll never see home —I'm ript up!' holding his bloody hand to his stomach.

'Let me see where you're kilt, Casey. There is no murdher here, everybody kills everybody—that's the order.'

A ball struck one of his buttons, turned off, and ripped open the surface of his bread-basket from right to left without in the least spoiling his appetite.

Andrew Orrell, one of my chums, was playing 'hide-and-seek' with a French voltigeur amongst the trees. I told him he would get a lump of lead that would stop his rations if he exposed his long legs to this rifleman any longer (he was all legs and a long Lancashire tongue), and very soon was he hit something like poor Casey. The ball broke a trousers' button, turned off its course, which was intended for the 'bull's-eye', went through his flank, and lodged at the backbone. I took out my penknife to cut it out, but he made such an oration, I knocked off surgery, and went to my own business. He was carried away, and came back all right in three months.

Lieutenant Ball had a narrow escape. A ball meant to go right through his head, was turned by the scale of brass on his cap, opened a furrow across his forehead, baring the bone and passing away on the other side. Poor A. B. C. (Allen Bellingham Cairns) was wounded, not badly; yet he died afterwards. I got his watch and key—the latter as a remembrance—no reminder like a watch-key. I have used it ever since, upwards of fifty years, and it is as good as new still and, I may say, it has ever since been a nightly remembrance of my old comrade.

It was wonderful the multitude of extraordinary wounds that men received. I felt a curiosity in their examination, attending with the surgeons at times (it was the profession that I was first intended for, so many of my name being eminent men in Scotland). Wounds in the feet and in the groin were the most painful and dangerous. Lieutenant G— had both his eyes shot out. Lieutenant C— narrowly escaped the same dreadful calamity; the ball passed close under the eyes, breaking the bridge of his nose, and spoiling his beauty., I have seen men wounded in every part of the human frame—some wounds most extraordinary and severe—and yet the men recovered. I should hardly get credit for the relation, if I enumerated them here.

Chapter Twenty-One
Spoils

The morning of the 22nd of June displayed the extent of the spoil which the runaway Frenchmen left behind them. There was a scene rarely to be equalled, for many leagues about Vittoria—the wreck of a mighty army, and plunder accumulated for years, torn with rapacious and unsparing hands from almost every province in Spain.

Waggons, and cannon, and caissons, tumbrils and carriages of all descriptions, upset and deserted, a stranger melange could not be presented to the eye. Here the personal baggage of a king—there the scenery and decorations of a theatre—war stores and china ornaments, all sorts of arms, drums, trumpets, silks, jewellery, plate, and embroidery mingled in strange disorder. Here were wounded soldiers, deserted women and children of all ages imploring aid and assistance and seeking protection from the British—here a lady upset in her carriage—in the next an actress or a *femme de chambre*; sheep, goats, and droves of oxen roaming and bellowing about, with loose horses, cows, and donkeys—everything in lamentable confusion.

Camp followers were dressed up in the state uniforms of the King Joseph's court; the rough class of women-kind, drunk with champagne and Burgundy, and attired in silks and Paris dresses once envied, perhaps, in a palace. The pride of France was, indeed, levelled with the dust after this signal defeat.

The greatest part of the enormous baggage and plunder was grabbed by the people who had the best right to it, viz. the Spanish peasantry following up our army. The sword of the King was secured, and a marshal's baton was sent by Lord Wellington to the Prince Regent, who returned the compliment by sending him a baton of a marshal of England. Oceans of women—wives, actresses, and nuns—were captured, but no padres that I heard of. All of them were treated with respect, and allowed to follow their husbands and sweethearts as they found opportunity.

A week or ten days were wholly occupied collecting the wounded and burying the dead, in a fashion, just as they fell. Men were found alive on the wild field the ninth day, where they dropped in obscure places. Having crawled to some waterpool they existed, but they were few.

Carts were in constant motion carrying away from the hospitals dead men and amputated limbs—a scene of anguish to look on—the pale, shattered, desolate, blood-stained, helpless forms of soldiers, so very lately in fine health, marching along for six weeks in joyful glee to meet a sudden death and no grave. Our saw-bones were not prepared for so much practice coming on them all of a heap, and hundreds died for want of medical care and hospital comforts. No fault due to our medicals; they worked away day and night at their trade like good ones.

When the battle began, my old friend Dr. Maurice Quill was in his proper place, in the rear of his regiment. He deposited his carving tools under a tree in charge of his hospital sergeant, and crept along in rear of the troops until he saw the men begin to fall, when he ran away back as hard as he could tear to bring up his mule and the apparatus. Doctors wore at this time cocked hats and feathers, and were not easily distinguished at a little distance from the general staff. As he went at speed on one side of a hedge, a general officer with his aide-de-camp came galloping up the opposite way.

The General cried out, 'There's an officer running away, stop him. Halloo! sir, where are you going to?' No answer. Both wheeled about their horses, and called loudly to stop. 'Stop, sir!' cried the General, 'and give an account of yourself and your name.'

'No, no,' said Quill. 'I'm off; seen enough fighting for one day,' and ran on. The General got furious. A court-martial at least crossed his mind as he pushed on after the fugitive, the stiff fence between them.

'Give your name, sir!'

'Oh, never mind my ugly name, everybody knows me. Your life's not worth a dollar this blessed day. Go to the front and be killed if you like—everybody's being killed but myself—oh, such slaughter!' speaking all this time over his shoulder and running like blazes. On he went at full speed, pursued by his enemies till he came up to what he called his tool-box (the hospital panniers), told his hospital sergeant to load the mule and move up quickly to the front, while he got out a few things for immediate use, and then right about face and away back as hard as he could tear.

'Oh, I see it all now!' said the aide-de-camp, "tis that wild fellow Maurice Quill—always up to some drollery in camp or quarters'; and with a hearty laugh they galloped away.

Chapter Twenty-Two
To the Pyrenees

At early dawn on the 22nd, our bugles sounded the assembly. Men and officers might be seen emerging from ripe wheat-fields nearly as high as one's head, and from behind hedges and ditches and trees, until all the living got under arms to pursue the retreating enemy. About mid-day, as we were marching over the hills, there commenced a fearful thunderstorm. I was riding alongside of my friend Masterman (who gave me the two dollars at Estramos when I was so hard up on my way to Lisbon). Poor fellow! he was struck dead in a second of time, by the lightning—his horse was also killed, the hair of his head was scorched, his watch-chain cut in two, and the little steel screws inside were extracted. The full force of the forked thunderbolt passed right through him. I was so electrified that I lost all power of holding my horse, which ran away with me downhill in fright. My knees shook and trembled, my hands were useless. I lost all power of holding or guiding my little jennet, although I managed to keep the saddle, and gradually recovered. The glittering arms of so many men, no doubt, was a great conductor for the lightning—several were knocked down, but none killed. The regiment halted for a melancholy hour, the pioneers dug a grave under a big olive-tree. Poor dear Masterman was rolled up in his blanket, and left behind! Awfully sudden: on this summer's morning to lose his hold of life, and pass away!

Alas! poor Masterman, so kind, so gentle—such a favourite with all of us; mourned for and deeply regretted; escaped from the battle of yesterday, today snatched off in a moment. But in those days nothing more sure than 'battle, murder, and sudden death'.

We followed after the runaways, leaving the great fortress of Pampeluna blockaded by the Spaniards. It was the key of the kingdom. It had a garrison of 3,000 men and an able commander, but was not victualled for a very long siege. When the French got well into the hill country, they gathered up some pluck, rallied, and contested every mile of ground. By this time they had lost all their guns, 150 brass cannon. We had many sharp affairs with them, so very unwilling were they to leave Spain. But we never let them out of sight until we drove them right over the Pyrenees. They robbed and plundered everywhere *en route* to make up their losses; but murder and even worse crimes were combined with plunder. Our own men were very expert at times, just looking into houses along the way for a *parlez-vous* or a loaf of bread. On one occasion, opening a press, the poor man of the house fell over on the top of a big grenadier, quite dead. Perhaps he had taken refuge in the press from the marauders, who, as they looked in, found the poor fellow hid there, and ran a bayonet through him.

Women and young girls were found on their own hearth-stone, outraged and dead. Houses were fired and furniture used for hasty cooking, as our army passed along. Such is war! We had the last brush with these vagabonds on 30th June, *i.e.* on the Spanish side of the Pyrenees, while skirmishing in the wood up the hills, General Sir William Stewart, a brave and gallant officer, who had been wounded in the leg at Vittoria, was at our head, with a pillow between his leg and the saddle. He was here wounded again, for there was no keeping him out of fire—just like Picton, that old hero, always foremost in the fight—and so he now passed us, going reluctantly to the rear, held on his horse by two soldiers.

'Sorry to see you wounded again, Sir William,' we said.

'Never mind—never mind me, gentlemen. Take the hill—take the hill,' was his reply.

He had a lisp, and spoke quick. I can see him now, distinctly the bravest of the brave, cool and collected. He was always cheered by the men when at any time riding through the camp. We took the hill, of course. In doing so, Brigadier Sir William Pringle was badly wounded, shot right through the body, but he ultimately recovered. Our Major (Worsley) tumbled over. Some wag cried out, 'There goes a step in the regiment'; but he was out in his reckoning, for the gallant Major was on his legs *tout de suite*. His horse was shot in the head and dropped like a stone; a bullet ruffled one of his epaulets, but left him all right for another day.

One of our sergeants, a fine young fellow, said 'We must not leave the Major's saddle and bridle behind, I would rather carry it on my back.'

While stopping to unloose the girths, a French rifle-bullet hit him in the mouth, and took away his lower set of teeth quite handy. No dentist could have done it in half the time. It was an ugly wound, and deprived him of all acquaintance with hard biscuit for many a long day. I do not know what forty or fifty thousand of our men were doing at other points on our left. They may give an account of themselves, or some clever cove may do it for them. I must stick to my own people, General Hill and his division and endeavour to immortalise myself by writing a book. There are, I believe, different ways of leaving a name in remembrance, and I honestly confess that I have no talent for book-making, and am one of the least qualified for such an attempt. I am therefore ready to be 'kicked, cuffed, and disrespected' by the press and by the public for such presumption.

At sundown, on the last day of June, we fired our last

shots into the skirts of the *Parley Vous*, as we slashed them over the hills into their own country, while they carried along with them the curse of a whole kingdom!

We went down and encamped in the beautiful valley of Bastan to have some rest after our two months frolic across the country. The men wanted washing, and shaving, and patching, and darning, scrubbing up, and a bit of polish for the next fight. I continued to sleep under a tree; my bed was the royal sack filled with ferns, dried grass, chopped straw, or anything soft that came to hand. In my good days I rode about the country, into the town of Alizondo, and made my acquaintance with the mountain passes, hamlets, and houses of the Basques—a quiet, primitive, honest people, like the Swiss, fond of their native hills, and speaking a language distinct from Spanish or French. They were very active and intelligent, detesting their French neighbours, who plundered them as they did everyone else. They wore wooden shoes, and a facsimile Kilmarnock bonnet.

Three of us chummed together. Having a horse, I was considered the grand forager for the mess. I sometimes got a loaf of bread for a dollar, some milk and honey. The chestnuts were large and ripe, they flourished on great shady trees above head. My horse ate them raw; we preferred them roasted or boiled; they filled up chinks, and were a good stand-by, better than the acorns in bivouac at Salamanca.

The Basque lingo was most difficult to get hold of. The only word I could retain in memory was '*house-quack*', *i.e.* the bellows, which I often borrowed to blow up our fire under the chestnut tree. I drilled our servants to be very civil to these people; they would lend us anything they had.

'Well, Tom, what did you say to the lady of the house?'

'O, sir, I just seyd, plase mam, yill you lend us the housequack, an' she handed it out at onst; but I forgot the name av the fryin'-pan, ours is goin' in holes, an' beint of any much use.'

In fact, Tom was always brushing the bottom of this old frying-pan with a sprinkling of water to burnish our shoes, which had a wonderful effect on leather, and was a tolerable substitute for Day and Martin.

A chaplain was now in reality sent out from England, and attached to Farmer Hill's division. My regiment was here alone, and his reverence came to perform Divine Service; twenty minutes was the regulation time. A square was formed, the big drum placed in the centre to do the duty of a reading-desk. The parson entered, made for the drum at once, got one leg up, when the big drummer made a rush, caught him by the tail, and pulled him nearly over, saying, 'You'll be through it, sir; the only parchment in camp.' The poor padre thought, he said, it was to elevate him in reading the service. No one, of course, could keep his gravity during this scene. I remember the text very well—in *St. Luke iii. 14.* There went a buzz through the ranks. The men knew very well they were six months' pay in arrears, and their daily bread was killing and slaying their neighbours!

The 7th of July was one of my very worst ague days, but turned out afterwards a day of rejoicing, thanks to our enemies. I was lying under an apple-tree in the beautiful valley, *hors-de-combat*, in a hot fit, my head splitting open, as I thought, with pain. The day was extremely hot, which only aggravated the malady, and increased my sufferings. All of a sudden the drums beat to arms, the bugles sounded the assembly, and the men hastened to the alarm-post, and the order of march was—up the mountain as fast as we could go. I joined my company, and dragged myself along with difficulty, faint and weary with pain and debility. There was in those days a chivalry, an *esprit de corps* amongst officers and men never to be absent if possible when there was a chance of a brush with the enemy. It was a point of honour not to be detained by any trifling illness, and so I stuck to my trade as usual. When we got up to the, tableland, we met the French advanced skirmishers, and renewed our acquaintance in a very unfriendly way, by knocking over a few of their riflemen. The compliment being returned, both sides went to work, and the matter was who would live longest under a shower of lead.

Their supports came rapidly up, swelling their ranks, while our brigade, 28th, 34th, and 39th decreased in numbers. We fired kneeling, to take down all the birds we could. Still, so overmatched were we, that the combat became extremely doubtful. Plenty of help was coming to us, but never came. A whole division of ours was lost in a fog, crawling uphill in another direction to take the enemy in flank.

Wellington and his staff came up, but the fire was so brisk and the heather about their horses' heels so torn up with musket-balls, he said, 'This won't do, we must get away. These regiments will be sacrificed.'

The fog saved us. It came on so thick we were all soon rolled up in a cloud of darkness. The fire continued at random, the French still groping their way. We heard them distinctly talking and getting nearer and nearer. Being formed in line, both ranks kneeling, we gave one loud cheer and a volley, which took the shine out of them for half an hour, when they commenced another fire at a greater distance, all their shot passing over our heads. This waste of powder and ball lasted till eleven o'clock, but we never arose from the sod until daylight next morning. The fog then cleared away, and we saw the strength of our opponents far below, going home to breakfast!

When the fog rose in the morning under a bright sun, we discovered the extent of our loss. Lieutenant Ball, who was hit on the head at Vittoria, was here badly wounded.

Some fellows were always being hit, while others—a few others—went through all the war without a scrape. The wounded were groaning on the heather all night, and not a drop of water within our reach. They always suffer extremely from thirst, and their cry is, 'Water for God's sake!' I remember drinking more water on an occasion of this kind than I had done for a month previous.

My servant followed me yesterday to the fight, seeing I was rather shaky at the start, and got his arm broken by a musket-ball; my two left-hand men had their legs broken. We had many wounded; the dead were left where they fell, and being myself first for escort duty, I got charge of all wounded in the brigade to take them to the hospital at Alizondo. The only conveyance for these poor cripples with broken legs and arms and shattered shells, were some mules sent up by the Commissary. Two men were placed on each mule, with their broken limbs bandaged up in a way and dangling down. No help for it; no cart-roads in the Pyrenees, and the poor fellows were groaning with their sufferings all the way.

When night came on I got my cavalcade under cover of an old cattle-shed I happened to spy out a little out of my way. The assistant-surgeon got them dismounted as quietly as possible, and laid some upon dry ferns. We had nothing to eat or drink; not a spoonful of water for the dying men. I could not sleep for their moaning and groaning all night. I could not see them nor help them in the dark.

When the morning was welcomed in, I found that many had passed away to the promised land; the mortal part was left where the spirit took its leave. We had no means here to bury the dead. We got to Alizondo on the second day of torture and suffering, and glad I was when I delivered over my charge to the chief saw-bones and was allowed to depart for my home, which I always considered to be under the colours of my gallant corps.

On the 7th I was roused up in a fit of ague. I went into fire unexpectedly; in the excitement I forgot everything. I lay out under a cold damp fog all night; the ague took flight and never returned during the war! Some fellows said that it was frightened out of me! Maybe so. I wish it had been frightened out of me sooner. I have had some severe shocks of it afterwards in the East and West Indies, and other climates, but I know how to treat it without any medical advice—quinine!

I found my old corps with the flags flying on a tableland half-way up the Pyrenees, and they were here 8,000 feet high.

Chapter Twenty-Three
Fighting in the Mountains

General Hill settled his headquarters in Alizondo. I was invited to dine with him by my old Captain Egerton, his chief aide-de-camp. A great day for G. B.! I had a better dinner with him afterwards in Belgrave Square! But he was always so kind and hospitable, so desirous to make one at home and talk over the old campaign, it doubled the agreeable pleasure of meeting him when Commander-in-Chief, with Egerton as his private secretary. I lost two good friends when they finished off their campaign.

The 2nd Division was encamped in the valley of Bastan, detaching a brigade in advance up the hills; from this brigade a regiment went forward a long way up (relieved weekly). This advanced corps gave the pickets and outposts, which were planted on the very tip-top of the Pyrenees. The view was very grand, and and the climate up there charming. France lay right in our front, and as we looked down below, there was the French army in camp quite visible, and their drill going on as in a barrack-yard. 'Plenty on 'em (as one man said) arter all the whackin' of late.' To the left the sea and the ships—a glorious sight once more. On the extreme right the *magnum mare*, but quite out of view.

The 34th, being the advance corps for the week, gave the pickets on the 24th July, commanded by Captain Moyle Sherer, a vigilant and distinguished officer. He had three Subalterns, H--n, R--l, and P--s. On Sunday morning, the 25th, at dawn of day, the picket and outposts were suddenly attacked by an advance of French sharpshooters.

The signal-gun was fired, when we got away up hill as fast as we could (the men never went on a parade at any time but in heavy marching order, just as if they were never to return to the same spot). But the pass up was narrow, steep, and tiresome, the loads heavy, and the men blown. We laboured on, but all too late—a forlorn hope; our comrades were all killed, wounded, or prisoners. The enemy had full possession of the ground. Some 10,000 men were there, nearly all with their arms piled, enough of them arranged along the brow to keep us back. It was death to go on against such a host; but it was the order, and on we went to destruction; marching up a narrow path in file, with men pumped out and breathless, we had no chance.

The Colonel is always a good mark, being mounted and foremost. He was first knocked over, very badly wounded. The Captain of Grenadiers (Wyatt), a very fine handsome man, being next in advance, was shot through the head. He never spoke again. My little messmate, Phillips, was also killed. I thought at the time, what a sin to kill such a poor boy. Seven more of the officers were wounded, the Adjutant, severely hit, tumbled off his horse and was left for dead (more about him hereafter).

We persevered, pushed on, and made a footing notwithstanding our disadvantage, for the men were desperately enraged and renewed all their exertions to be at them with the bayonet, but in vain. We kept our ground until we were minus, in killed and wounded, some 300 men and 9 officers; some slight wounds were never returned. We did not think it very warlike to notice every skelp one got when little harm was done. But this little point of modesty was a mistake, found out too late, for at the conclusion of the war every officer who had been returned as wounded, was compensated from a great fund raised by the usual liberality of the English people, and many were well recompensed for the loss of a little claret or broken bone.

Different regiments scrambled up the hills to our relief as fast as they could.

The old half-hundred and 39th got a severe mauling. Then came a wing of the 92nd and opened a flank fire on the enemy, while we moved over to another hill, got our men left, and commenced a cross fire. The 92nd were in line pitching into the French like blazes, and tossing them over. They stood there like a stone wall overmatched by twenty to one, until half their blue bonnets lay beside those brave northern warriors. When they retired, their dead bodies lay as a barrier to the advancing foe. O! but they did fight well that day. I can see the line now of the killed and wounded stretched upon the heather, as the living retired, closing to the centre.

Every regiment that came up lost its quota, and the French increased as the battle went on. We had two six pounder guns up here for signal, to give warning. Richardson, self, and two other lads made an effort to turn them to salute the French, but a few rifle-shots stopped our play, so, for fear they should go over to the other side, we wheeled them round and at the word 'Let go' away they went rattling down the mountain with great velocity, perhaps never to be seen again. We 34th for the last hour had been amusing ourselves in comparative safety, picking off our friends in the distance, when a very large column came down upon us to stop our play. There was but one escape for us now—to run away, or be riddled to death with French lead. The officer commanding, a brave man, saw how useless it was to contend against such a multitude, gave the word to retire at the double, and, away we went down hill at a tearing pace. I never ran so fast in my life! Here the French had another advantage, rather a cowardly one. They kept firing after us for pastime. Every now and then some poor fellow was hit and tumbled over, and many a one carried weight over the course, *i.e.* a bullet or two in the back of his knapsack.

We were now broken and dispersed. Our bugles sounded, few heard them—some too far way!

The old corps was severely handled. We hoisted a flag at the bottom of the hill, Freeman blew his well-known blast, and all that heard the sound rallied here. Up another hill we scrambled, and passed the night among the heather. Hungry, cheerless, and thirsty, I would have given a dollar for a drink of water. Lieutenant Simmons had his horn full of brandy slung on his back going into action, and was about to rejoice over it just now, but alas, the bottle was empty. A musket-ball played one of those practical tricks one hears of after a big fight. One passed through the horn during the row, and let off the brandy without any notice. Simmons knew that he had been slightly wounded in the side, little knowing it was a cow's horn saved him! Our sergeant-major found his arm very stiff about the crook, as he said; no blood, nor mark of a shot-hole. He pulled off his jacket and found a ball lodged in his elbow-joint, which had run up his sleeve in this playful way. A young officer was shot through the nose, which, as he jocosely said, made him sneeze a bit! Every part of the human frame in one or other was riddled with shot, and many wonderful escapes were talked of that night—were there any thank-offerings?

In the middle of the night, a horseman nearly rode over me bawling out for a doctor.

'What's the matter now? Who's dead that you want a doctor in the dark?'

'Sir W. Stewart bleeding to death, they say.'

'Sorry for it, he's always getting bled by Frenchmen's lead. Call louder, all the saw-bones are asleep,' and he passed on. Soon after an orderly dragoon came thundering amongst us in our feather—no, in our heather beds—calling out for a guide (all such orders in the dark were circulated by a loud call).

'Where to, France or Spain?'

'No, sir, Alizondo.'

'Well, I know the way, I think, in the dark, if that will do.'

'All right, sir. Will you come with me to the Quartermaster-General?'

'Yes, lead on, I want to warm my legs, the dew is heavy, and I feel stiff and powerless. I feel very like the Irishman's gun, that wanted a new stock, lock, and barrel, all in rags, and my barrel empty. Have you got any water in those holster-bags of yours?'

'Not a drop, sir. Not a grain of barley for my horse all day, nor a pick of a ration for myself, being the whole day mounted and riding about with orders. The men got a great slashing today, sir. I see them coming down the mountains in hundreds wounded, forby what on 'em were left behind doubled up, an' the whole country below like a mixed fair. The Commissary, artillery, baggage, and wounded all jammed in that narrow road, trying to get away; but we're near sir.'

He called out, 'The Quartermaster-General said that Sir Rowland Hill wished to get his division out of the hills the very shortest way into the valley by daylight.'

'Do you know any path?'

'O, yes, I think I will steer the column out of this darkness,' and took my place and led the way down curving goat-paths, clear away into Baston before sunrise.

I had the personal thanks of the dear General, and moreover dined with him. We had a sheep's head for dinner, the first I had ever seen decently cooked, a dish I have patronised ever since, as it makes a first-class curry.

A month had only passed away since the battle of Vittoria,

and here the French stood triumphant on the Pyrenees, for all the passes were forced on the same Sabbath day! The truth was, the Emperor superseded his brother Joseph (it was but mockery to call him King), gave the command of the army to Soult, with orders to reorganise it, and, when prepared, force all the passes in the Pyrenees, assault Wellington, drive him back into Spain, relieve Pampeluna before it fell, and be quick about it! It can't be denied that his first efforts were successful. We all felt it to the bone, and the men were vexed and disappointed.

The French army came down after us very cautiously on the 26th, but declined battle, endeavouring to get round our flank, a movement well matched by General Hill. We retired and took up position on the 27th. They came on, looked at us, but would not engage in any war game that day either. Our great chief was engaged during all this row with the siege of St. Sebastian, which he left in a hurry, and came up to us in the nick of time. He was always the right man in the right place; all honour to his glorious memory. He saw at a glance the object of his adversary, and put his army in motion. Soult was pushing on for a great victory to restore the fortunes of France. At a racing speed Wellington rode for Sauvoren, and seeing the enemy close at hand, is said to have dismounted, taken a look at Soult, as pointed out to him by a Spanish spy, pencilled a note on the parapet of the bridge, despatched it by his only staff-officer present, Lord Fitzroy-Somerset, and rode up the hill alone. He was at once recognised by our troops, who raised a triumphant shout of gladness. The cheering swelled out loud and long as it ran through the line from corps to corps, and became that appalling shout which the British soldier is wont to give upon the day of battle, and which the army of France never heard unmoved!

Our Field-Marshal stopped in a convenient spot, conspicuous enough to be seen by his troops, so as to let them know that he was on the ground. It is said that he fixed his eyes on his formidable enemy, and speaking as to himself said, 'Yonder is a great commander, but he is a cautious one, and will delay his attack to ascertain the cause of these cheers; that will give time for the 6th Division to arrive, and I shall beat him.'

The Marshal Soult made no attack that day. Nevertheless, there was some hard fighting at different points between the detached divisions of English, Portuguese, and the French, but now for another battle, which caused mourning and lamentation, pain and sorrow.

Chapter Twenty-Four
Pampeluna

Early on the morning of the 28th July, our chief formed his army in order of battle in front of Pampeluna, in the midst of rugged hills, craggy rocks, and rivulets, and there waited the pleasure of the French Field-Marshal, who sent on his legions with all the ardour and determination of a warlike people, to win this day and let his troops once more into Spain to regain their reputation. Both sides were soon engaged, and under a biting fire. Both fought bravely, but nothing could stand against the ragged red-coats of old England, when they met their late acquaintance on fair honest ground, with any sort of equality. Both armies were jealous and vexed, the French having been whacked out of Spain, and the allies having met with some reverses of late. Now was the time, this was the day to decide a great and final triumph—ay, for a kingdom.

For two miles and more a storm of fire raged along the line. The ground was uneven, rugged, and hilly. Strong posts were taken and retaken with the bayonet. It was what the Duke called 'bludgeon work'. Charge succeeded charge; each side yielded and recovered ground by turns, yet all the noble valour of French effort was of no avail.

Wellington brought forward, at a critical moment and at full speed, the gallant Enniskillen and the Northampton regiments (27th and 48th), who came with a rush from the hills against the crowded masses of the French, rolling them backward in disorder and throwing them down the mountain side. With anything but child's play, these two regiments fell upon the enemy three separate times with the bayonet, and although their charge was irresistible, lost more than half their numbers. A great slaughter was going forward along the whole line of battle, the cannonade furious. Every man held his life in his hands, to dispose of it to the best advantage for his own country.

A French brigade made a great dash up a connecting hill. Our gallant Somerset regiment (the 40th) waited in stern silence, and with unwonted patience, until the enemy planted their feet (with their *En avant*) on the very summit, when the war whoop of charge was given. The whole mass was almost completely broken to bits. Away they went at the double, a tempest of lead following their heels. Four times this assault was renewed, the French officers, caring for nothing but victory, dragging and driving on their weary and exhausted men to win or die! The thundering shock and cheer of the British soldier ever prevailed in these days, and, at last, with their ranks thinned, heartless and fainting, hopeless from failures, the French gave way, having lost two Generals, a great many brave officers, and 1,800 men in this part of the battlefield.

We had less sanguinary play against Count D'Erlong in another position. Every regiment drew a prize that day. The British soldier is a disciplined biped. Discipline is the sure means of conquering, without which bravery is useless, and ours was an army always ready to go into action, not to be driven. It was the difficulty to keep them back and restrain their impatience, game-cocks as they were, and as they proved themselves this day, and every day.

Soult was still very powerful, and kept up the ball day after day, hoping still to gain some advantage against Wellington. Of the danger and intricacy of this hill country, in manoeuvring and fighting an army, no one can form anything like a true idea. A formidable enemy might be concealed within a mile and the sharpest eye not know it. The great chief, with an escort, I believe it was said, of the 43rd, went out to reconnoitre in the hills, and dismounted to examine his maps. A sergeant, who was sent up the hill to look out, had not been there long when he discovered the French winding round the side of the hill, where our Wellington was sitting. One of the men holding his caballo (horse), Sergeant Blood, as his name was recorded, came flying down the rocky hill like a deer, calling out, 'The French! the French!' He might have called out, 'The Philistines are upon you, and what a prize!' But the Duke was mounted and away at full gallop in a moment, not without a shower of bullets after him by the disappointed Frenchmen. There were spies in both camps, and they well knew the whereabouts of the grand prize! There was hard fighting and plenty of broken bones on the 29th and the following day. Then Soult went off in retreat the way he came, the whole British army at his heels like terrier dogs, snapping at him round every corner.

When our Colonel was wounded on the 25th, shot through the knee-joint, the agony was so great he was put into a house by the roadside. His servant and the doctor (Murray) alone remained with him. The French advanced that day, and hearing that an English officer lay wounded there, Count D'Erlong, the General commanding, went in to express his regret and to assure him of protection and quiet. He placed a guard at the gate and a sentry at the door, with orders that no one should be admitted while his army was passing that way—a noble trait of generous feeling. But the Count was always a kind-hearted, good soldier, and respected his enemy. It was said at that time that he and Sir Rowland Hill, now in direct antagonism, had been at one time school-fellows.

It so happened that my regiment, in following up the retreating French army, passed along the same road over which we had retired, and coming to the little house in which the Colonel had been left, and hearing from his servant at the gate that he was alive, the men gave one unanimous cheer, which so unnerved him that the doctor came running out to stop a repetition of such kindly feelings.

He said, 'The Colonel is doing very well; with the only help I had (one servant) I cut off the leg to save his life. The French behaved admirably, only asked the Colonel's parole, would not take mine, the Count saying I had only done my duty. And now keep quiet,' he said, 'he knew the cheer came from his own men, but another like it might destroy life, he is so nervously excited.'

In due time he recovered, went home, and was exchanged for a Colonel of the French. He was appointed Governor of Pendennis Castle, married a wife, and had three sons in the army, all Colonels.

Chapter Twenty-Five
War in the Passes

We pushed on to the pass of 'Donna Maria', where the French made a stand, and we had a big fight, the 34th leading. A thick fog prevented our pursuit, there was a small victory, and a loss of 400 *hors-de-combat*. Soult kept on his retreat through the mountains, and Wellington kept his eye upon him like a hawk. But there is nothing certain in war—a great chance was lost, and here it is recorded. The French Marshal had got into a deep narrow valley and halted. The Duke gave strict orders to prevent fires being lighted, the straggling of soldiers, or any indication of the presence of our troops. He placed himself amongst the rocks, from whence he could observe every movement of the enemy.

Our troops were ready to cut them off, when unluckily a few marauders entered the vale, and were instantly carried off by some French horsemen, when their whole column beat to arms and marched away. Thus a few plundering vagabonds deprived the great chief of the splendid success he had in his eye, and saved the French from a terrible loss. However, they were pressed hard, and although they got out of this prison, their chains hung round them. The pass was narrow, the beaten army was great, vast numbers of the wounded were carried by their comrades on their shoulders, while their baggage impeded the march, and all got mixed in extreme disorder. Prisoners and baggage fell at every step into our hands. Men fled from their broken and confused ranks up the hills for safety, being all sorely crippled before they got out of this trap, to fall into another where they were wedged in a narrow road with steep rocks on one side, and the river on the other. Indescribable confusion followed. The wounded, thrown down in the rush and trampled on by the cavalry, were calling out to our people for quarter, while very many were supported along, carried on branches of trees, on great-coats clotted with blood, and gory stained sheets taken from the cottages. Wretched sufferers! brave men would not, did not fire upon them, and so they straggled along out of this labyrinth. The Spanish General Longa, as usual, did not attend to his orders, or the retreat of this part of the French would have been entirely cut off—but the prize was lost.

General Hill pursued his old friend D'Erlong to the pass of Maya. Pitching into his people as we went along, we helped them over the hills here, 8,000 feet high, and halted on the old battleground on the 1st of August, being absent only eight days! Our dead lay there just as they fell, only most of them stripped naked, decomposed, and swelled up to a vast size. Some had the appearance of being dressed in fine white muslin shirts, the skin inflated and raised up from long exposure to the air—the medicoes may understand it, I don't. The vultures had been here, they always followed the armies—dirty birds of ill omen. They begin their feast with the eyes, and sometimes leave bare bones!

I was for picket, and had to pass the night in the midst of this loathsome company of horrible perfume and decaying humanity. Going my rounds, I was continually stumbling over old comrades, and would then roll my head up in my cloak, and lie down amongst them for half an hour or so, jump up, and tumble over another ghost!

Next day we had all the dead covered with sods; graves were impossible on that rocky ground.

The 2nd Division now encamped on the tip-top of the Pyrenees, along the ridge from Maya to Roncesvales. Sir

Rowland Hill pitched his tent amongst us and kept a sharp look-out against another surprise, for a surprise it was in July, and no mistake. I lost two of my messmates for whom I was very sorry, particularly for the joyful, rosy-faced lad Phillips. But there was no real grief for any one beyond a week or two—all a shadow that passed away. Their effects were sold by auction. We bought their clothes and wore them, and they were sold again perhaps in a month, being once more part of the kit of deceased officers killed in action.

The mountain sides about the pass of Roncesvales were covered with thick woods; trees were felled, and log-houses built at every point where an enemy might approach, and we slept with one eye open. I formed a new alliance, got into another mess of three, our assistant surgeon, Robert Simpson, president! A fine, handsome, clever young fellow, and a general favourite in and out of the regiment. He was afterwards surgeon of the 13th Dragoons and 7th Fusiliers. I was still the active forager for the mess, being mounted. Our batman always took good care of my horse, which, with others, was always kept with the baggage when there was any fighting going on. Poor Tom Tandy, my old servant, was killed in one of the late battles. He knew my ways and winks, he knew how to forage in safety, and just the sort of fellow who, if hard up, could live on the smell of an oil-rag for a day or so. I got another intelligent sharp fellow, who knew a sheep's head from a carrot, was only sober when he could get nothing to drink, but never got into a scrape. Along with the rations, he sometimes had a present of a duck, or an old hen from the 'valley below'. Pigs were few hereabouts, but the fairies would be kind at times and shove a little joint under the walls of our tent after night!

I used to ride into Alizondo, and get back the next day with anything I could pick up. A dollar a loaf for bread was the usual price asked and given, sausages and pork were scarce and dear, and no wonder after a French army passing twice through this little pretty town. Every man in a French army has the organ of destruction just over his eye; what he can't use he will destroy from pure mischief.

The weather was charming. We had little to do, little to eat, no books, and led a monotonous life. We would pass hours rolling stones down the mountains; it sometimes occupied three or four of us for an hour engineering at a great rock to get him up on the right end for a start. Once in motion, nothing could stop its heavy velocity. It dashed through the forest trees amputating great limbs and branches, making such a row as it passed away, and leaving an echo which traversed the forest and deep glens even into France.

We had very advanced pickets posted in chain-links down the hills on to the French border within pistol-shot of the *Parley-vous*. I always led my horse down to keep me company, and get him some good grass feeding, when on this duty. There was a picket-house, where the men kept up a roaring fire. I took the sergeant out in the middle of the night to visit the outposts. One of the sentries was gone; we halted to listen for any sound or voice. We knelt down and put ears to the ground, when we heard voices in the distance and gradually approaching us. It was dark; they knew where our pickets were posted every night, and thought to catch us asleep.

I said, 'They may make a dash. Fire at once in the direction, and alarm our men at the house.'

'Wait, sir,' he said, 'a moment. Let them come a bit nearer. Now, I hear them pushing through the bush'; and he fired.

All the other sentries immediately fired at the moment. There was no other result that we could tell than the words, *'Ah, grand diable—'* and all was quiet.

My horse lay down beside me at the fire amongst the men, like a Christian, and we had no other adventure that night.

At one of these outposts our sentries had disappeared in the night three times, and always at the same place. They were good intelligent soldiers, not at all likely to desert. Many surmises and opinions were advanced about this mystery. I recommended double sentries one night to be planted close to each other—one of them to have his ear to the ground frequently, to catch any sound or movement. The place was very quiet and retired, by the side of a goat-path amongst the rocks, and the night was dark and late. One of the sentries jumped up from the ground, where he had been most attentively listening, and whispered to his comrade that he heard a little rustling amongst the leaves and low brushwood. There was no wind, all else was calm and quiet. They now stood together a little more retired, round the edge of the rock breast high, and waited this coming ghost, as they said, with their flints fixed.

The men's names were Murphy and Styles.

'Don't you hear a noise, now,' said Murphy, 'just like a pig smellin' for acorns?'

'I do, and I think I see something crawling up here, like a bear. Will you cover him, and fire? I'll keep my shot in reserve—hush! It approaches slowly, on all fours, and crouches down.'

'I see it,' says Styles, 'it's a bear. Cover him well, and knock him over.' And over he went at the instant.

Both men waited a little—one to reload, and then cautiously advanced with fixed bayonets. The game was dead as a door-nail—and what was it? A Spanish spy (perhaps) in the French service, dressed up in an old bear-skin, armed with a sort of tomahawk, short spear, and a *cuchillo* (Spanish knife). No doubt the same wild beast that carried off former sentries, who might not have been so watchful on their solitary outpost. We supposed this wild beast might have had a reward for every red-coat he caught alive. It is certain none of our men were found, dead or alive, after we missed them, and again, the French had too much of military honour to engage in anything so unworthy of their noble character. The advanced sentries were always doubled in future.

Twelve battles had been fought within the last seven or eight weeks, in which the French lost 15,000 men, and the allies 12,000. The streams of blood were deep, and everything seemed to recoil at death but the soldiers in this war. There were deeds of valour achieved by hundreds of British officers, within the last few weeks, that would astonish the soldiers of any other nation in the world. Wellington himself declared that 'he could go anywhere and do anything with the army that fought at Vittoria and in the Pyrenees'. Yet those officers were entirely neglected by the influence of cold aristocratic pride, injustice, and partiality. Promotion went too often by favour. Court influence, political intrigue, or Horse Guards' interest.

I remember riding sixteen miles one day, through slush and mud, over the fetlock at every step, for no other purpose but to get a real dinner at St. Juan de Luz, and bring home something for our mess. The posada was crowded, horses and mules stood jammed together in the stable as close as they could pack. I bought a good bundle of forage for my poor tired horse, but his neighbours right and left had eaten two-thirds of it, for they had nothing provided for them. I had myself a wretched apology for a dinner, and a corner of the floor to lie on, without bed or blanket. One would desire neither if he meant to have a snooze; a soft plank is preferable to a lively mattress.

This was the Duke's headquarters. My companion on the ride down to the coast was the senior Lieutenant of the 11th Regiment, a man of long and good service. There was a death vacancy, and so fearful was he of being passed over, that his object was to see the Duke and to present his letters of recommendation to secure him a step which was his legitimate right. Many brave men were driven out of the service by tyrannical injustice. They could not brook the system of being passed by and purchased over by boys from the nursery, who stayed at home and never smelt powder. Army tailors had wonderful interest in those days!

Chapter Twenty-Six
Nivelle

All military men who have seen much active service have no doubt had many opportunities of witnessing the dash and courage of the British soldier. How, when the hour of danger approaches, his anxiety to meet it increases, and how, still more, he will court danger, although duty does not call on him to face it. I remember one striking example of the latter.

It was a practice permitted in regiments to send a steady noncommissioned officer down to the coast to bring up what good things he could purchase for the officers. He had his list, a bag of dollars, and a couple of mules, with a pass from the commanding officer. On one occasion, when the great siege and butchery was going on at St. Sebastian, a sergeant named Ball, belonging to the 28th or 'Old Slashers', was on his way with a party for this purpose. Hearing the guns, he pricked up his ears like an old hunter, persuaded his party to follow him, lodged his trust—some 2,000 dollars—with a Commissary, took a receipt, dashed on, joined the storming party, survived, reclaimed the money, made his purchases, and returned to his regiment without any boasting or bravado. Insensible to fear or danger, this was the stuff our men were made of!

We changed our quarters or camp from Maya to Roncesvales. It was late when we pitched our tents in a beech wood. All tired, we lay down upon the sod, and were soon asleep. The first object that caught my eye in the early dawn inside our dwelling, close to my nose, was the two feet of a dead man with his toes up.

'Hallo!' I cried, 'whose ghost are you, my friend? And how came you here?'

'O, begad!' says my comrade, 'here is a fellow's head under my pillow of ferns! We are in some graveyard where they don't bury the dead; we have pitched our tent in the dark on the late battleground, amongst the dead.'

'By Jove!' says Captain Darcy, a rollicking Irishman, 'I didn't pitch at all. I saw a fellow snug asleep in his blanket, and lay down quietly at his back to keep myself warm. When I cleared my eyes this blessed fine morning, who was it, do you think?—don't know? A dead man, sir, without rag on his back, enough to frighten a donkey!'

Many of the old Buffs and 20th had fallen here on the 25th of July; we knew them by their buttons. They had not been buried; we had them all covered up and changed our ground.

We led a monotonous idle sort of life here. We had no fine view into France, as at Maya. It was a thick wood before and behind us, outlying pickets were our only amusement!

At Roncesvales, a very small town on the highway from Spain into France, there was a posada, a sort of inn or caravansera, full of muleteers and *ladrones*, followers of the army. I rode down there one day to dine at the *table d'hote*, put up my horse and stopped an hour to regale the inward man on a sausage and some rice, oil, and *vino tinto*. I smelt strong of garlic for three days afterwards—so I was told. Going into the stable for my horse, he was there, but the saddle and bridle absent without leave. I called out the patrone, kicked up a dust, but the innocent landlord knew nothing about it. I persevered in my search, twenty or thirty fellows watching me. At last I discovered the treasure up in a loft, covered over with chopped straw. I saddled my jennet, rode away in triumph, but never to return to dine at Roncesvales.

Our brigade returned to the Maya pass, and we had the pleasure of looking down upon the French army in the distance becoming again organised and getting ready for action. We overlooked their camps and saw their drills going on. They could only see our flags flying above them, the old 'flag that braved a thousand years the battle and the breeze'.

October came on, and with it the snow, which buried us all up for some time. We were frequently dug out of our tents of a morning by the pioneers. My old Captain, who never loved fighting, had gone away somewhere to take care of himself, and I had no one to cash a bill for me at 30 per cent.! My best donkey died in the snow, and my mule was stolen one night when I was on outlying picket. I sat down now in real grief, and could have cried with vexation.

Misfortunes seldom come alone. Here was I in a fix; I had paid sixty dollars for the mule and forty for the donkey. There was no remuneration, a dead loss of one hundred dollars to be made up from my pay, 6s. 6d. a day, minus income tax, which was never forgotten to be deducted from our paltry pay, which was now again five months in arrear. I could not bear this double misfortune with a patient endurance, and fear that I was very stormy about it. But, *cui bono*, what can't be cured must be endured; it might have been worse. Had we got a sudden order to move, I should have had no choice but to leave my little baggage behind me, but the snow kept us fast. Provisions became very scarce; bread, six pounds, thirty reals, or about 6s. a loaf, when we could get one. Anything else to be had was equally dear, and no wonder when such a multitude of locusts were on the ground.

Towns, and villages and hamlets of white canvas were to be seen everywhere, all alive and red-coats and blue. The Spaniards were not particular in their dress—a coat, like

Joseph's, of many colours, seemed most in fashion—and with a ration of beef (raw), or any bit of plunder, stuck on the bayonet, they passed on in their own rollicking, independent way, more like banditti than soldiers.

There was always some officer being killed, or disposed of, which caused an auction sale of effects, and so I bought another stout baggage animal on tick. We always got credit until the next issue of money, or by a bill on home, which was more acceptable. Somehow, my money never lasted its natural time! As Paddy said who lost the despatch on the road, 'It eloped out of his pocket'.

We had many severe snowstorms at night, and one day in particular, a hurricane that floored every house in the town, church and all. The commanding officer's marquee was called by the wags the church, the rest of the tents the town. Huge branches were torn from the trees and whirled through the air like feathers. Thin streams swelled into torrents, and dashed down the mountain ravines, rolling great stones with a mighty clatter. The melting snows increased into rivulets and waterfalls, where so very lately we could not get so much as would fill a teapot. In the distance we could observe the sea, in terrible commotion about Bilboa and Santander, where many fatal disasters occurred. This very rough weather did not last long, and glad were we to see the heather green once more. I always had a good bed since I picked up the royal sack at Vittoria. Stuffed with leaves or chopped straw, it was in-valuable; yet I was doubled up with rheumatism for nearly three weeks, and unable to run in a foot-race, sweepstakes, a dollar each, ready money, the second in to save his stake. Very few could beat me in this sport, and none with the pole.

Pampeluna was still holding out. Being the centre of a ring, no one could get out, no one get in. And so the question was only a matter of time, and many were the bets about its fall. The most common was, 'Give me ten guineas and I will give you a guinea a day until the town falls', or, as the case might be, five, six, or seven guineas.

Pampeluna, the key into Spain, did fall; not before the garrison had eaten up all the prog in the city, as well as every horse, dog, donkey, cat, rat, and mouse that they could catch. They held out bravely until starvation compelled a surrender, and no fortress being now in our rear, Wellington prepared to enter and visit our old friends in la belle France. We left our snow-capped mountain homes on the 9th of November, and descended the hills to cross the border, just to see what the *parlez vous* were doing there so long, and soon found that they had been very industrious since July last, fortifying an immense position on the Nivelle, extending all the way to the seacoast, about sixteen miles.

We were, under General Hill, on the right of the army, the Duke on the left, fighting in the mountains. For weeks past there was a continued struggle going on to dislodge the French from strong posts they had occupied in the intricacy and labyrinth of this hill country. Other Generals, brilliant and brave, commanded the centre, and there lay the promised land before our eyes. Who will cross the border and live?

Few people, I fear, ever thought of danger or death, heaven or hell. Death was too familiar to be looked on with terror, and made no impression. I never saw a Bible nor do I remember ever seeing anyone read the Bible, although that is the book, a sure guide on our way to eternal life. We never thought that the time was short and the soul precious, where the man spared in the battle of today was killed on the morrow. I don't say that men did not pray, but I never saw but one on his knees. Yet here was a palace for prayer—pray in the open air, "Tis God's palace'.

> *To kneel remote upon the simple sod.*
> *And sue in forma pauperis to God.*

What could be more acceptable? Or what place more appropriate for a soldier? But soldiers were not looked upon in those days as parts of humanity, although wasting their lives to keep the people of England in possession of their wealth, their homes, and firesides.

Corporal punishment went on everywhere the whole year round. Men were flogged for small offences, and for graver crimes flogged to death—a thousand lashes were often awarded by courts-martial. I have seen men suffer 500 to 700 lashes before taken down, the blood running down into their shoes, and their backs flayed like raw red-chopped sausages. Some of these men bore this awful punishment without flinching for 200 or 300 lashes, chewing a musket-ball or a bit of leather to prevent or stifle the cry of agony; after that they did not seem to feel the same torture. Sometimes the head dropped over to one side and the lashing went on, the surgeon in attendance examining the patient at times to see what more he could bear. I did see, with horror, a prisoner receive 700 lashes before he was taken down. This was the sentence of a general court-martial, carried into effect in the presence of a brigade, for an example.

We had certainly some very bad characters sent out to fill up gaps in the ranks of the army, sweepings of prisons in Great Britain and Ireland. But such punishments were inhuman, and I resolved in my own mind if I ever had the chance of commanding a regiment I would act upon another principle. The time did come, and I did command a gallant corps for eleven years, and abolished the lash. Kindness is the key to open the human heart, and with that key I reformed the worst characters. It does not always tend to reform a man by bullying and abusing him before his comrades. I often made a deeper impression by taking a bad character into my room privately, speaking to and admonishing him in a sort of friendly way, appealing to his better feelings, and with a promise to forget all the past. In this way I reformed one of the most drunken characters I ever met wearing a red coat. He became the Quartermaster of a militia regiment afterwards, a teetotaller, and a most intelligent, useful officer. His name was Murray.

On the evening of the 9th of November we bivouacked on the broadside of a heather brae (out of sight of the French outposts not far away) to eat our supper of whatever might be found in the old haversack. Little and good would have been acceptable, but it was generally less and bad. We lay in groups and talked of the morrow, and of a great battle sure to come off, for which the two game-cocks of England and France were long preparing.

'Now, Tom Eccles', I said, 'good night, and mind that if you run your jolly red nose into danger, as you always do at the first flash of fire, we will miss you tomorrow evening.'

This was a most excitable, young, thoughtless Irish officer, who had fought through the whole way up to the present Lord Mayor's day. He had nearly lost one of the colours of the regiment in Albuera by running far in advance of the battalion while fighting in line. The staff of the flag was cut by a shot in his hand, while he was loudly cheering on the men. Nobody could hold him, he was always in the front of the battle. When the morning signal-gun fired for our advance, the whole army already being under arms, loaded and ready for action, we went forward by divisions, brigades, and regiments, according to the nature of the ground and previous arrangements. Skirmishers to the front. In ten minutes or so the dawn was lighted up by the flashing of great guns and small-arms. The fusillade ran down the line like wildfire. Poor Eccles, always foremost, was riddled to death with French bullets. We never saw him more.

Several points of the enemy's position were assailed

at the same time, and some of their intrenchments and redoubts taken at the point of the bayonet; but these were minor works in advance, which were only taken after a sharp resistance and loss on both sides. They were beaten back to their stronger position, well defended and guarded by batteries, breastworks, and plenty of cannon, with brave men and gallant officers ready for death or victory. '*En avant*' was their continual cry, and '*Vive Napoleon*', '*Vive l'Empereur*'. Our shells and round shot kept them uneasy on their ground, while our men were advancing in their old formidable way of renewing acquaintance with 'Johnny Crappo', as the soldier red-coats so often called them.

It was hard work charging up these sloping hills, receiving a heavy fire in the face, and losing men at every step; but if a certain number were destined to fall, the survivors only got the more excited in strength, agility, and resolution, feeling determined to win, and never looking behind. Oh! how clearly I can look back and see that day and noble deeds of valour displayed on both sides. That gallant *chef de bataillon*, leading on his men, waving them forward with his cocked hat at arm's length high in air. He rode far in front and cheered them on, while our shot were rattling amongst their legs.

Our men were saying, 'Well, I'm blowed if I like to knock him over, he's so plucky.'

'Ay, Bill, but you see he must come down, for he wants to be killed.'

'Faith, and I'll make him leave that,' says a big Irish grenadier, 'or he may be riding over us,' when down he tumbled off his charger as dead as a stone.

I was really sorry for him at the moment, but he was madly brave. All this was but a preface to the great battle of the day then only beginning.

Ninety thousand of our troops, with ninety-five pieces of artillery, and 4,500 cavalry, descended to fight this great battle. I believe the French army were less in numbers. They had more cavalry. They were of one country and one language, while the allied army were a mixture of English, Spaniards, and Portuguese, the Spaniards never to be relied on in the moment of trial and danger. The French too were fighting in France, for France, and on a very strong position which they had been fortifying for three months, so they had no disadvantage.

The river Nivelle formed a semi-circle; both flanks of the French army rested on that river. In the centre of their commanding position many hills and mountains were strongly fortified with all the skill and ingenuity of Frenchmen. I believe such defensive posts could not be wrested from our old red-coats, but our fellows took them all that day under a most tremendous fire, and an avalanche of great stones which rolled down the hills amongst them and made them jump about like buck-goats, as they expressed it.

General Hill, with 25,000 men, threw himself on the left flank of the enemy, and made his attack. General Sir John Hope assailed the right, while the great Duke forced the centre after a most severe conflict. We had redoubts—batteries, abbatis, and deep intrenchments in our front, with a determined and most formidable foe well planted behind them, shooting fast and thickly as we advanced. Their skirmishers were all driven in by this time. The battle now thickened fast, but no one could see very much of this brilliant fight beyond his own regiment or brigade. Indeed, at times I could see nothing from the obscurity of powder-smoke.

As we advanced, the red-glare flash of the cannon, the bellowing of the guns, and the white puff far to our left, showed us that death and destruction were extremely busy, but that the fight was going on in our favour.

I was on the right, with Lord Hill, and when the

moment arrived to make the grand coup, he made a flank movement, getting on the French left, while the centre of their position was penetrated by one grand and tremendous effort. The day was ours—they began to retire. Once the chain was broken, nothing could stop the current of their speed. Away they fled; d—l take the hindmost; nobody wished to stop them! Our fellows forgot their fatigue in the moment of victory, hurried on and after the enemy with a cheer and a volley, and many fell at the eleventh hour. I confess I was not sorry to see them give way, for we had enough blood and brains on the sod for one day, our loss being 2,690 officers and men, 2 Generals, the late Lord Strafford and Sir James Kempt, wounded. The loss of the French: 4,260 men and officers, 1,200 prisoners, 1 General killed, 50 cannon and their field magazines taken, to swell our triumph. And great swells we thought ourselves that day!

We passed on through their lines of defence, where they had been so long domiciled. Their huts were extremely neat and comfortable, many had their green blinds over their little lattice windows; their neat little fireplaces, bedsteads of green boughs, shelves for their prog, and arm-racks, so like the natty Frenchman in camp. We found their rations uncooked, and plenty of onions and other vegetables, which were transferred tout de suite into our haversacks *en passant*. We pressed on with a running fire after them until sundown. Then we gave up the chase, stretched our weary limbs on the November sod. We turned out the contents of our larder—a Dutch cheese, onions, biscuit, cold ration beef, and a little rum—and finished off the breakfast, dinner, and supper all at a go, went to roost, and thus ended another chapter of the war, as recorded in history.

It was marvellous how quickly the dead, and often the wounded, were stripped on the battlefield by the camp-followers of the two great armies—an unhallowed trade, and no stopping it. I remember nearly stumbling over the bleeding body of a young French officer rolling in the dust, speechless in agony, and stark naked! He was very handsome, well formed, and from his light moustache he had not numbered twenty years. A ball had passed right through his body, poor fellow, and his end was near at hand. I had wished him out of pain before I passed on. Close by him lay one of his rough soldiers, also stripped naked, showing a terrible and fatal wound, and rolling over and over in the dust, for the November day was warm and the ground very dry.

Many young officers have an opportunity at times of distinguishing themselves in battle, while others are more careful of life, or may not have the chance. Two or three I may name whose memory will never die as long as the history of the Peninsular War is read. Lieutenant-Colonel Thomas Lloyd was killed today at the head of the 94th Regiment. He was a valiant officer, skilled in knowledge and of great experience. He predicted his own fall, as many often do before a battle, without any abatement of courage. When he received a painful and mortal wound, he remained on the ground watching the fight, and making his own observations, until death closed his eyes where he fell, at the age of thirty years.

Another young fellow, a simple Lieutenant, about nineteen, bearing many wounds, in person very slight, and so very handsome that the Spaniards thought him a girl in disguise, fell on that day. So vigorous, active, daring, and brave was he, that the old soldiers watched his looks on the battlefield, and followed wherever he led, and obeyed his slightest signal in any difficulty or danger. Edward Freer was well known. One of three brothers, who all died in the service, he had also that presentiment of death in the coming battle so often felt and expressed by military men. He was pierced by several balls in the early part of the morning while storming what was called the Rhune rocks amongst the hills. Old soldiers wept for him, even on the battleground, when they heard his fate!

After five hours' hard fighting about the above rocks, where poor Freer was killed, the Spaniards cowed, and hesitated to attack an outwork, or abbatis, behind which a very strong regiment of French were firing as hard as they could load. Lieutenant Havelock, of the 43rd, who was then on the staff, a young officer of a brave and fiery temper, could not resist this opportunity of showing the Spaniards the shortest way how to quench this murderous fire. He took off his hat, called upon them to follow him, and putting spurs to his horse, at one bound and a dash cleared the fence, and went headlong amongst the enemy. The Spaniards followed, shouting and hurrahing for '*El chico blanco*'. This one shock broke the spirit of the French, and sent them flying down the hill, the Spaniards in their turn paying them off as fast as they could load, and crying out, '*Viva el chico blanco*!' (Long live the fair boy) for he was very young, very fair, and very brave. The Spaniards would have fought well had they been led in this gallant style, but their chiefs were too haughty, proud, and selfish to admit English officers to command in their service. Not so the Portuguese. Every regiment, I believe, was commanded by an English officer, who obtained a step of rank as he passed from his own corps into the other. So a Captain in my regiment became a Major, with Major's pay in the Portuguese service, and his superior rank was confirmed after the war. The Portuguese army was always well and gallantly led, fought well, and ranked next to the English troops in all ways.

Marshal Beresford was their chief, and he sent his troops into the field well disciplined and well clothed, with an *esprit de corps* not so well understood amongst the *Espanoles*.

There was more genuine heroic pride amongst the ladies of Spain than in the ranks of the army. I remember a beautiful Castilian maid looking from the balcony of her house on to the square where some Spanish troops were again preparing to take the field after a severe defeat and a run for it. She said, '*Los Engleses son bravisimos, pero nuestro general es una vieja*' (The English are very brave; but our general is an old woman), and concluded by saying or speaking through those bright expressive dark eyes, 'I will never marry a man who will not distinguish himself in the army of Spain and for the honour of his country!

'Bravo, senorita', I said, 'you are worth fighting for.'

'*Gracias, senor*', she replied, '*a-Dios! hasta la vista,*' and she tripped lightly away.

I saw her afterwards enjoying the fashionable but barbarous delight of a bull-fight, in the square where all the beauty and fashion of the town assembled, seated in the balconies and eager as we are on our race-course to see the 'Derby'.

There were a multitude of people below enthusiastic for the sport. The different entrances into the square were secured by wooden bars fixed into the grooved stone sides. A bull was driven in, who faced the audience with dignified simplicity. He was hooted, jeered, pricked with spears, and taunted for his patient forbearance, but declined a quarrel with his adversaries on any terms, and was turned out in disgrace. Another of the tribe was driven into the arena, a very stout, fierce-looking fellow, with short, sharp horns, a fiery eye, and full of mischief. Some one gave him a prick of a lance behind, when he made a sudden rush forward, caught a fellow on his horn, and pitched him up in the air like a sheaf of corn, then stood with a defiant look, pawing up the ground undecided what to do next. I was in the crowd, expecting safety amongst so many, and, as I supposed, out of horn's length, when this wild beast made another charge, cleared all before him, and took a bit out of my best holiday white trousers behind with the tip of his horn. My conscience! if I did not run for it, and soon found myself high up in a balcony, never to be seen again amongst such wild beasts in a bull-fight!

This poor beast was now driven to utter madness by his tormentors. Several men were carried away wounded, perhaps dead. Two horses were killed, and dragged out of the square amongst the cheers of the people above, the ladies waving their handkerchiefs. This was quite delightful!

The square was now clear of all but two expert horsemen with spears and scarfs, and two or three regular professed bull-fighters on foot, armed and dressed in the same way. They were the most expert, active fellows I had ever seen. When the bull made a charge at one of them, he threw a red mantle over his head, and slipped aside. Now a horseman attacked him with his spear, and there was another rush head foremost, horns nearly touching the ground. It was surprising the dexterity with which the horses were managed so as to escape; however, they were occasionally ripped up! The poor beast was foaming at the mouth, with wild bloodshot eyes, but still powerfully strong, when the matador, the great leader in these games, jumped on his back while a mantle had been thrown over his head and horns, and gave him the *coup-de-grace*, and 1,000 voices gave consent to this finale with no end of bravos, and the now happy bull was dragged away. This is the national sport of Spain; so enjoyed by all classes of the people, from the *grandee* to the *pizanno*, and is it less cruel than the cock-fighting of England, now happily abandoned?

Our supplies now became very scanty indeed, and

there were symptoms of discontent in the camp, for it was reported that some Commissaries had a league with speculators down at Bilboa and St. Ander, and used the public mules for getting up luxuries for sale at a fabulous cost. But our great chief appealed to the military honour of the army to be patient and firm, and the supplies would come in as usual in a few days. The Duke had only to make an appeal at any emergency to his ragged red-coats, and they would go through fire and water for him, ay, to the death. It was hard on those fighting fellows to be so long in arrear of pay, and to have their rations cut short. I paid sixteen dollars myself for a pair of boots, brought up from the coast, and everything else was equally dear.

Sir Thomas Picton told his Commissary one day that if he did not find rations for his men, he would hang him on a tree. The Commissary became very indignant at this insult (as he termed it), and went off to Lord Wellington to complain. After hearing the whole story with wonderful complaisance, he said, 'Did Sir Thomas really say so?'

'Yes, my Lord, those were his very words.'

'Very well, you had better get the rations, or you may be sure he will keep his word. I can do nothing for you; good morning!'

The Commissary returned and found the rations for his brigade.

Maurice Quill, joking on the parade-ground one day after the men were dismissed, said, 'Who will ride over to headquarters and smell out some prog? I used to get a sheep's head upon tick once a week from our butcher, but I never see head nor horns now.'

'O,' says Tom Higginbottom, 'I suppose you're going to dine with Lord Wellington.'

'Well, I might do that same and do worse. As for you, Mr. Higginbottom, you begin to crow very loud that you have got the use of your Irish pin again. The next time you get a crack on the leg perhaps I may give you the chance of a pension by taking it off! I am going over to headquarters, and if any of you sporting fellows are inclined for a bet, I'll stake ten dollars that I will see Lord Wellington and borrow ten dollars from him before I come back, and more than that too, I'll bet other ten dollars I will dine with his Lordship.'

'Done, done, done,' shouted (with loud laughter) many voices.

'Win or lose, my coves, the money to be paid the next issue of pay,' and the bets were booked.

Saw-bones, as the Subs called him, was full of adventure, and loved a joke whatever it cost, but this day's excursion and his bets would have shut up any common-place man in the camp. However, he mounted his mule in a most confidential cut, as they said, and we saw him really off; whistling along to bear his courage up, turning over in his mind, no doubt the sort of reception he was likely to meet from so great a man as we all justly thought the Grand Duke to be.

Riding up valiantly to the quarters of his Lordship, he gave a thundering knock with a big stick at the door, and asked if the Duke of Wellington lived here.

'Yes, sir,' said the orderly, 'here is an aide-de-camp coming. May I ask your business, sir?'

'I wish to see Lord Wellington, if he is at home.'

'His Lordship is in the house, but too much engaged to see anyone today. I will take your message to his Lordship.'

'No, I thank you, if I can't see him today, I will wait until tomorrow.'

'Something particular, perhaps, you wish to say in private.'

'Precisely so.'

'Well, step in, and I will see what I can do for you.'

Away he went and told his Lordship that 'a Dr. Quill

was below in a state of anxiety, and would not take any denial, came a long way to see your Lordship, and could not go back until he delivered his secret.'

'Well, well, show him up.'

After some bowing and scraping—'My Lord,' he said, 'I am the surgeon of the 31st and have come over to pay my personal respects, and to see your Lordship, and—'

'Yes, yes (cutting him short), how are you all getting on in the 2nd Division, many men in hospital? You must get them out, we will want them all by-and-by.'

'Indeed, my Lord, I was going to say, that we are badly off for hospital supplies, and no money to be had. I think I could get many restoring comforts for the invalids that would put them on their legs if I might make bold enough to ask your Lordship for a loan of ten dollars until the next issue of pay, when I will return it with a thousand thanks.'

'Very well, very well, Mr. Quill, you shall have it. How far have you come today?'

'O, indeed, I have rode seven long leagues on an empty stomach, and there's not a bit of an inn over the whole country where a body could get a morsel of dinner.'

'O, well, if not too late for you, stay and have some dinner before you return, we dine at six. Good morning, Mr. Quill.'

Quill's eyes opened wide and joyfully at this invitation. He was punctual to the six as he said. All his wit and humour came to the surface. He kept the table in a roar of laughter all the evening until he retired with his ten dollars and his Wellington dinner, got a shake-down with his friend the aide-de-camp, and his whack of brandy and cigars. He got safe home next day and claimed his bets. He told his story honestly and gave his reference. But there was no question about it, everyone knew him to be as upright and honourable as he was eccentric and surcharged with mirth and glee when others were desponding.

Some impudent fellow asked him one day why he had exchanged into the 31st. 'O, just because,' he said, ' I wanted to be near my brother, who was in the 32nd.' That man was shut up, and asked no more questions.

The weather became very wet and rainy about the end of November, but we happened to get under cover in some hamlets near the Nive, hard up too for provisions, and no money. The French had cleared the country of everything as they retired, like so many locusts. I had three articles that I could pawn, or pledge, or exchange, and they must go: an old half-crown, and the silver fork and spoon I bought in Lisbon.

The half-crown had been given to me when a lad, by a kind, good old lady who said at the time with great simplicity, 'My dear, as long as you keep that, you will never want money!'

She was right, but I thought I had kept it long enough, and exchanged it for an old hen, the mother of many a brood. The fork went for one loaf of bread, and the spoon followed in a few days. An iron fork was always my abhorrence, but there was a necessity.

Bread was dear; when an old Spaniard said to our paymaster, 'I can't eat your gold, senor, I'm starving myself.'

The money offered was sufficient to buy a baker's shop well stored.

Chapter Twenty-Seven
We Enter France

The French crossed the Nive—it was now our line of demarcation. We planted our line of pickets along the left bank, while they did the same on the other side, with an understanding between us that there should be no hostilities without due notice. The river was narrow, but rapid in the rains. We kept watching each other carefully day and night, yet were good friends.

We conversed with the French officers across the stream. They told us of their many escapes in action, pointing to bullet-holes in their head-dress, and why they had retired just now, 'just to collect all their forces and be ready to return to Spain when the Emperor came down to take the command personally.' In reply, we told them how happy we should be to meet them all in Paris soon. This little badinage went on with good humour. We exchanged newspapers occasionally, rolling up a stone in one and throwing it over, and getting one in exchange.

On the very day that we entered France, the Spaniards lost no time in beginning their foraging excursions amongst the people and spreading themselves over the country, committing all sorts of villainy on their murdering excursions. They considered marauding, murder, and plunder their chief duty, now that they got into an enemy's country. The poor French people fled from their homes in terror after witnessing the frightful excesses of those wild and reckless fellows, whose country, no doubt, had suffered most fearfully for many years under the dominion of the soldiers of France—not from the peasants of Gascony.

Wellington marked his lofty character of justice in putting to death all the marauders he could grasp, and sent back into, Spain their whole army, save that of Morillo's division. Thus confidence was restored, everything was paid for, and a friendly intercourse established—much to our satisfaction and advantage.

Our men made acquaintance, too, with the French soldiers across the river. This being a permanent picket station, they built a hut here, which was added to daily until it became a water-tight, snug little dwelling, and a shelter from the rains. It stood just opposite a ford, with the entrance facing the French picket on the other side, There were stepping-stones of large size across, which were used by the country people when the river was low. One day they were all dry above water, and the next covered, perhaps, by a torrent.

Our fellows knew there was brandy in France, but the matter was how to get it. They made themselves very agreeable to their neighbours, calling out at times '*Bono-frances*', *Fromage, Cognac,* and *Tabac*, which seemed to be understood over the way, so they established a telegram when the river ran low, they subscribed their coppers, put them into a mess tin, gave it a rattle to draw the attention of the sentry, and without any arms in hand, one of the picket stepped down to the water, gave his tin another rattle, placed it on the centre big stone, calling out '*Cognac*!' and retired. By-and-by it was taken away, and returned in the evening full of brandy (not likely of the best quality). The relieving picket was let into the secret, and the trade went on for a while, but not so smooth as the stream, for the brandy-pot forgot to come back one day.

One Paddy Muldoon, a big Irishman—always very fond of a 'dhrop,' as the boys said—was very indignant at this 'thratement,' and watched an occasion to square accounts with the robbers 'acrass the wather.' Seeing the sentry put down his firelock for a few moments to go into the hut, he dashed across, laid hold of his arms, and, as the rogue of a *parlez-vous* stepped out, he gave him a clout on the head and brought his firelock over to his own side in pledge for the brandy-pot.

Soon after this feat the French officer on duty came down to the bank and called over for the officer of our picket, told him the true tale, and requested that the firelock might be restored, or the young fellow, who was but a conscript, would be tried for leaving his post, and severely punished.

A search was made in the hut, the musket found and restored. The French officer returned thanks, and Paddy was sent back a prisoner to the camp, where he was tried for the offence, found guilty and sentenced to a corporal punishment. He was a brave, dare-devil soldier, and his defence was honest and truthful.

He said, 'he only wanted back the money or the brandy, an' did not want to be done by any ov them frog-ating fellows, who he was chasing all over Spain for three years, and hoped the coort would consider his good service, and the next time he met this fellow, he might rely on it he would never see his firelock again.'

The punishment was remitted, and the brandy trade stopped.

The weather was now mild, but very damp and rainy. The winter had really set in and kept us under cover until the usual time of turning out, one hour before daylight, when all the troops, were on their respective alarm-posts until dismissed and we could see a white horse at a mile distant. This was the most disagreeable part of our war game. On the 8th of December there was a great Stir of cocked hats and orderly dragoons galloping about—a sure indication of a move. The men dived into the secret at once, and began to fix their flints and look to their ammunition. In the middle of the night we received orders to be on our alarm-post earlier than usual in the morning.

The women were all astir in a moment, lighting their fires 'to have a dhrop ov tay for their respective warriors, jist to warm their hearts before plunging into the river, bad luck to the French.'

Well did they know our line of march, and were always in the way; but this intended advance bothered them. How were they to cross the river and follow the troops, against a positive general order? The ladies assembled around a big fire on a dark winter's night to discuss this point. Mother Skiddy, Brigadier-General of the Amazons, so called, addressed the meeting.

'I have the weeest donkey of you all, an' I'll take the wather if I'm to swim for it, and let me see who's to stop me, Bridget Skiddy, who thraveiled from Lisbon here into France. If Dan falls, who's to bury him? God save us! Divil a vulture will ever dig a claw into him while there's life in Biddy, his laful wife. Now, girls, you may go or stay.' and so she began to saddle her ass.

The troops were now assembled in perfect quiet. No drum nor bugle was sounded—not a word was spoken—all as still as death, waiting the signal-gun to make the rush. The outposts on the riverside had their orders not to take any advantage of the enemy when, just at dawn, bang went the first cannon. The French were under arms in a moment. Our pickets on the river-bank gave them the signal to clear off. They took the hint, got out of the way a little, halted, and formed up on the defensive. Bang went another gun, and now the field-day began. Our men had slung their pouches behind their necks, resting on the pack, to keep their powder dry, as the river was swollen. The grand rush was now being made under cover of our guns. We took the stream; some killed and wounded went away with the current, for the French kept up a fire on us now, which was quite lawful. We made good our footing on the right side, fought on all the day, and calling the roll at night, we found there were many widows.

The passage of the Nive being successfully made by our division on the right, there was hard fighting along the left of the entire position, and a desperate attempt made to repulse our whole army. It was known at the time that Soult had written to the Minister of War to expect good news very soon, Wellington's army being divided by the river Nive. Lord Hill's division, being now situated in an angle between the 'Nive and Adour', was cut off from Wellington. It was very unpleasant, to say the least of it, and required great caution and brave hearts, resolute and determined, to keep our ground.

On the 10th Soult attacked Wellington in front of Bayonne with 55,000 men and thirty-seven guns. The ground was very unfavourable for fighting—ugly weather and swampy land, rough and rugged—it was always cheery enough fighting over grass fields and churchyards on a sunny day. The Light Infantry and Rifles liked the tombstones, they said they were such a steady rest for a pot-shot, and a good shield!

The great Marshal Soult got a thrashing today after all his boasting and expectations, but it cost the Duke 1,200 men, 2 Generals *hors de combat,* and 300 prisoners. However, to balance the account, the French loss was considerably more. Moreover, a whole regiment of Nassau and Frankfort came over to us, their Prince having abandoned the Emperor Napoleon in Germany. But there was no end to this quarrel. We were all fighting again the next day, when there was a trifling loss of some 600 men a side. The 12th was also a bloody day in our army. Death was busy from dawn to dusk, and that was only preparatory to the following day, the 13th December 1813, when Soult tried his grand coup upon General Hill.

Chapter Twenty-Eight
Saint Pierre

On the night of the 12th the rains swelled the Nive, carried away the bridges, and left us cut off from the rest of the army, between the two rivers, with less than 14,000 men and officers, and twelve guns. We had a front of less than two miles of ground, which was rather in our favour, the enemy not being able to deploy their overwhelming force. We (28th, 34th, and 39th), occupied a plateau on the left, the Chateau of Villefranche being just in our rear.

The morning was ushered in with a wet, misty fog. We had no time for a mouthful of breakfast, shook the rain out of our blankets, and stood to our arms. The fog continued heavy, covering the vast masses of the French dimly seen. Now and then, they appeared in solid columns like black thunder-clouds, as the mist rose spreading over a mile of ground.

Soult expected to trap our Farmer Hill and his little force by marching out from Bayonne and his intrenched camp with 35,000 fighting men, quite fresh, and forty guns, early in the day. The sparkling fire of the riflemen spread far and wide over the low grounds, and gradually crept upon us, while the thundering of parks of artillery shook the ground from river to river, but never shook the nerves of a British soldier. The French General Abbe pushed on his attack against our centre, with a force and determination difficult to resist, and gained upon us rapidly. The musketry and cannonade rolled for hours in our teeth. Regardless of all danger, the two armies now met each other. Neither would yield, and the artillery tore the ranks on both sides fearfully. We had hard work to keep our own against such long odds, 35,000 versus less than 14,000! Besides their forty guns against our one dozen of nine-pounders! Our brigade was let loose early, and we soon separated, on account of the ground, as we could thus do more work independently.

Colonel Brown said to the old 'Slashers', 'there they come, boys; if you don't kill them they'll kill you; fire away.' This was the longest address he ever made to his men. He never had but one book, and that was the Army List. He was a great soldier, very popular, and survived the war.

The Chateau of Villafranche, which was in our rear when we commenced operations in the morning, was well in our front before twelve o'clock, *i.e.* we had to abandon it to a superior force, and this caused our fellows to get furious. It had been taken and retaken several times today, but we held it at last. It was one of those fine old French family mansions that one sees sometimes peeping out of a wood elevated amongst the trees. It had been deserted, and left by its owners, well and substantially furnished in old style. The old ladies' armchairs, the library of the landlord, the young ladies' nicknacks, with all the beautiful china ornaments, etc., etc., were mashed up together. The feather beds, down pillows, mattresses and ottomans were stuffed into the windows for defence to resist incoming shot, and very sensible barricades they made. The cellars were not overlooked, and many thirsty souls were all ready to do full justice to the wines of Bordeaux, although preferring, as they always do, 'strong waters'. However, in this department they were generally disappointed, for some prudent officers were always at hand to knock the heads of wine and brandy casks and let them run.

We left this chateau now to camp-followers, the worst of all enemies (as it was no longer of use to us), and took ground to our right, to help a brigade of Portuguese who were fighting bravely. We were just in time to strengthen their hands to fight it out. Before we got up, we saw them twice charge their adversaries most gallantly with the bayonet. We pitched a flank fire into the *parlez-vous* and made them 'leave that', as Paddy said, when he fired at the French sentry.

'Did you hit him, Paddy?'

'No,' he said, 'but I made him leave that!'

The enemy now concentrated all their force towards the centre, to make the grand coup, and so we took that direction, keeping up the ball as we moved towards Saint-Pierre. This was a hamlet on, the main road, leading from the bridge at Cambo (across the Nive) into Bayonne. The French now attacked this point with three strong columns- the very key of our position; whoever kept this key was pretty sure to be master. We formed in reserve, a couple of regiments behind the houses, with a battery of three guns and a howitzer. A good deal of pounding went on below, and on both our flanks. Every point was attacked to weaken our force and keep us separate, their guns keeping up a terrific fire, knocking the dust out of Saint-Pierre, and ploughing up the side of the hill, thinning our ranks, and playing Old Harry, having no regard for life or limb.

We were now on the highway for a retreat or a victory. The latter was the choice of the British army, and nobly did they win it. Facing Bayonne, and on our right, an old British regiment was firmly placed in a very strong position, the right of that regiment resting on the Adour. As the enemy's main column advanced up the hill to the hamlet, they were annoyed by a flank fire from our left; but they persevered and approached within pistol-shot of the key of our kingdom! Just then our little battery opened a fire of grape into their ranks, which made a lane through their column. A few volleys of musketry, in their confusion staggered them grievously, and sent them pell-mell on top of their reserve, our guns plunging their shot into their ranks until there was a flow of blood down the great road. Yes, the blood was running in a stream!

A tremendous fire of artillery now covers the advance of another great column of the French, who are determined to have Saint-Pierre at any cost. With a cloud of voltigeurs in front and on both flanks covering their deep and dark masses, they steadily move up the incline.

We are prepared by order to be steady: 'Dead or alive, my lads,' said our chief, 'we must hold our ground.'

Every eye is fixed on this deadly mass, every nerve is strung. Like the gallant steed as he champs the foaming bit, ready for the charge, so was every man of ours in pain to be let loose. A howitzer, with a double charge of grape, went slap into their foremost ranks; then one tremendous cheer, that only British soldiers can give with electric fire!

'Hurrah for old England!'

'Ireland for ever and the Limerick lasses!'

'Bonnie brave Scotland, hurrah!'

'Hurrah!' from a thousand voices, as they dashed with the cold steel bayonets into the solid mass of human flesh before them.

Writhing and quivering humanity lay over each other now in mortal combat, steeped in blood. The cannon-shot from each side was crushing up the living with the dead and dying. It was a horrid sight, but not yet over. This broken column retired, and on the way lost considerably from our guns, which banged into them as fast as we could load. They went far away to the rear before they could reform, while another massive column took their place and came on.

The French always attacked in column. I think they were wrong, but they know their own business best, and upon this occasion gave us an opportunity of showing them an error, which they never acknowledged to this day.

This last black, dense, great body of troops came steadily on, encouraged by seeing our troops on their left give way, and losing their grand position, which might and ought to have been kept against very long odds. Lord Hill saw at once this alarming turn in affairs, and despatched part of his force to retard the progress of the enemy there or drive them back. We had not a man to spare. Another frightful and uncommon event occurred which nearly damaged our day's work. A brigade and a regiment were commanded by two nervous old officers who had no wish to be killed. They had most likely been reading that couplet in Hudibras—

He that fights and runs away,
May live to fight another day;
But he that's in the battle slain,
Will never rise to fight again.

Cowards die many times before their deaths—the valiant never taste of death but once.

They had a ticket of leave next day from the Duke, and were no more seen. I need not mention their names.

As this great column of French came up, they were first met by a discharge of shrapnel shells and canister shot, which did not slacken their pace over the dead bodies of their comrades that lay in their way. Saint-Pierre was the key, still in our hands; to lose it all was lost. The Highland Brigade was under cover, in waiting for them, headed by the gallant 92nd Gordon Highlanders, who led on the charge, colours flying, and their piper blowing out his national music to cheer them on. He was soon floored by a broken leg, but would not be moved, playing 'Johnny Cope' with all his might, while the blue bonnets, well supported, went into this mass with the bayonet and sent them back in utter confusion. This was to understand war.

We were also successful on our right and left. The French couldn't do it. They had enough for one day, and did not renew the attack. Two divisions which had been on the line of march since daylight now made their appearance in our rear, and formed in line of battle, but were not required. Our ranks were terribly wasted, nearly all the staff had been killed or wounded, as also three Generals.

Lord Wellington had been riding hard from the time he heard the first gun in the morning, and only arrived at the very close of the battle, and declared that he had never seen a field so thickly covered with dead. It was Lord Hill's own day of glory, and it was recorded by the celebrated historian, Colonel W. Napier, 'that five thousand men were killed or wounded in three hours, upon a space of one mile square'.

When the Duke rode up, he shook our chief by the hand, and said, 'Hill, the day's your own.'

Our men threw up their caps in the air, and gave one long loud, thrilling cheer, that echoed down the valleys amongst the retiring foe. And so ended the battle of the Nive, which lasted five days, from forcing the river on the morning of the 9th to the evening of the 13th.

Chapter Twenty-Nine
After the Nive

The days were short, and night closed upon the saturated field of blood before we had time to light our fires and cook the wretched ration dinner. But still, with our half-gill of rum, after so long a fast, exercise, and excitement, it was an acceptable banquet. It came on now to pour rain like fury, and the bivouac was anything but agreeable, particularly to the wounded, among whom there was a multitude of hurts (as the doctors called them), great and small, from the amputation of limbs to the scalping of heads! I don't know if I was thankful enough for my escape. I was not hit very hard and got off cheap. Three inches taller and it was all up. An inch makes a wonderful difference they say in a man's nose—life or death was today in the height of many a British soldier!

14th December. We sent in a flag of truce to the French General to say they might carry away all their own wounded men from off our ground, and we would bury the dead. We had no hospitals nor medicos to care for them, and as prisoners of war they were not worth their rations.

All was friendship and politeness now. Our offer was accepted, and a line drawn out between us. Some trees were cut down and laid across the high road into Bayonne. Our men collected all the wounded of the French, carried them down in blankets to this point, and handed them over. The sentries of both armies were planted along the line, not over six or seven yards from each other, as quiet and gentle as lambs! The hillsides were perforated with cannon-shot, some places like a rabbit-warren, and dyed with blood. Our little hamlet of Saint-Pierre was knocked inside out; but if ever the French got a decided thrashing, they might have boasted of it yesterday, in sight of one of their own chief towns. This 'labour of love', in presenting so many disabled and useless soldiers to their country, lasted some days, and no end to groaning and moaning until we had them all removed. Two or three nights exposed to the rains left many of the unfortunates in a pitiable condition, for they had fallen in sand-pits, amongst brushwood, and in nooks and corners out of sight. The rains continued to overshadow the scene of desolation all about us, and not a blink of the sun to cheer or warm the bivouac for many days, our baggage not having yet come up. We had no feather beds; the old pound of lean beef, a hard biscuit, and ration of rum our banquet; a cold sod and a shower-bath our dessert; hard times. But we survived them, to tell of yet more battles. Our sentries, and the French *ditto* paced at the distance of a few yards from each other, trying to converse a little in their respective lingos.

The officers kindly proffered their services in sending into Bayonne for anything for us that we required. We took advantage of their civility. I got a piece of cloth to make up a new Sunday pair of inexpressibles, very much required, and a bottle of brandy, for which I invested the few dollars in hand. The tailors were not all killed, and so I turned out very respectably dressed, but rather out of the fashion, in a week or so. We paid in advance. There was no mistake, everything came to hand about the hour appointed, and delivered at the outpost picket. The officers showed us the bullet-holes in their shakos and clothes; I believe we could do the same. They said we would all be back into Spain very soon. The reply was, 'Not before we see a little more of *la belle* France'; and really there was not the least animosity between us, and I thought it very unkind and inhospitable to have any more of a quarrel.

But the two great chiefs of the fighting cocks thought otherwise.

The truce ended, sentries withdrawn, we gave our friends warning to be on their guard, as we intended to pursue our campaign. They took off their hats with an '*Adieu, messieurs; au revoir*!' and it was not long before we met again in mortal combat. My regiment was left in the shattered hamlet of Saint-Pierre, to take care of itself and keep a sharp look-out to our front. Bayonne was just one league distant, full of French troops, and a whole army was concentrated in and about the city, holding fast their intrenched position, Sir John Hope in command. Vieux Monguere, a little town on our right, on a hill just above the Adour, where Lord Hill quartered himself and his staff, all jolly fellows. They were not long there before they got up an amateur theatre, and the drama went on as in Estremadura in Spain. Our dear, rosy-faced Farmer Hill entertained the whole *dramatis personae* at supper after the play. There was nothing about the war, except in some comic songs composed for the occasion, of how 'He (Lord Hill) leathered the French'. I had to walk home in the middle of the night, up to my ankles in mud, after the fun; but I had a pair of wonderful legs for hard work day or night. We had little to do now for a long time, but listen to the attack and defence about Bayonne—bellowing of guns and waste of gunpowder.

We had quite gained the confidence of the people. Everything was paid for. They were permitted to go into Bayonne with their sheep or their cattle as they liked, and soon found that the English were as equitable as brave, and that the word of a British General was sacred. All we seemed to want now was money, and a dollar was worth 8s.

The battle of the 13th was hardly over, when Mother Skiddy came into camp, mounted on her wee donkey, calling out for Dan.

'Has any ov yer seen Dan Skiddy? He's not killed or wounded is he by them vagabonds, bad luck to them. Sure I'd been up two days ago, only I was drowned crassin' that bit ov a sthrame, an' sure I've niver been dry since?'

'O, then, you're welcome home, Misthress Skiddy, how did you lave all behind you?'

'Och, is that you, Paddy Muldoon? Avourneen, it's me that's glad to see ye on your two Irish legs; I'm thinkin' you paid them off for the brandy.'

'Bedad, we gave them a great slashin', and not many of us killed after all. Will you let me take ye off your charger?'

'Is our Captain safe, and our two officers?'

'O, be gar they are, only Mr.B-- had a bit ov a scalp and a bullet through his cap in San Pierre there, but they can't touch him, or Mr. Norton in all the fights and scrimmages we have.'

'But where's Dan, tell at ons't?'

'O, indeed, he's run away wid a French lady he tuck in the battle.'

'An' he'll spake Irish to her,' says Mrs. Skiddy. 'But no more ov your blarney, where'll I find him?'

'Well, he's up there in the hospital tent wid a broken leg, and got off chape if they cure him; and there's Mr. Higginbottom wid another cropper beside him, and there's Sergeant—'

'O, worra, worra, that'll do, let me go, they're all kilt'; and away she went bellowing to the shambles.

We lost 300 officers the last five fighting days. Some of them had cut their way from Lisbon to be buried in France, but they were soon forgotten. They had their day of glory, and a bit of a churchyard fits everybody.

Wellington had his hands quite full. The intrenched camp before Bayonne was very strong, the weather rough and rainy for troops on the qui vive day and night close to a watchful enemy playing the sortie too often for one's comfort and patience, a game which ended by Sir John Hope being grabbed, wounded, and carried off to town quarters. A terrible slaughter of officers and men took place also on both sides, without any advantage being gained.

It was said, and I believe it was very generally recorded as true, that our patient, scientific, and gallant chief was abused and libelled by the Spanish Government, with all his army. Their hostility and growing enmity were no secret. We were all considered as invaders rather than friends. The insolence and duplicity of their Minister of War were obvious. All this ingratitude and savage conduct troubled the Duke's temper a bit. In fact, he had good reason to rebuke Morillo for allowing or permitting the Spanish soldiers to plunder in France, and to commit violence on the people, which he encouraged, from his savage, untractable, bloody disposition, hating English, Portuguese, and French equally. The poor French peasantry would have been entirely ruined without our protection. Sometimes they would take refuge in our camp or quarters with their bundles, even to escape from their own soldiers, and many of our own men were hanged for plundering them. I never could excuse our soldiers for committing any such excesses. But 'tis, true that they never saw their pay, and were half starved at times. Morillo, of course, sent a sackful of lies by every post to his corrupt, imbecile, prejudiced, ungrateful Government in Madrid for the snub he got from his superior. Spanish pride was touched with the pen of justice and equity, and Spain is jealous and revengeful.

No one complained if the Duke was severe in our own ranks; it was never without cause. It was said that he was cold and careless of his officers. Some discontented men may have said so, but the truth was, no one expected reward for doing his duty, unless for some very gallant and extraordinary conduct—such as the leading a forlorn hope, when a step of rank was expected. But there were a hundred chances to one against the daring heart that tried this game, yet they were never wanting to lead the way when required.

I sold my only donkey to raise the wind, and bought two nice little horses, on tick, at the sale of the effects of officers killed in action. A bill on England was always acceptable payment, or the next issue of money the same. This traffic always went on briskly, and in this way we were supplied with second-hand clothes! I was now ready for the road. My head-gear had something of a warlike appearance all right for a five-foot-nine man—a six-foot fellow, and he was a "gone coon."

We sent our wounded to Cambo, on the Nive, where an hospital was established. My poor friend Allen B. Cairns died there. He had been wounded, but not badly—what the doctors called 'a hurt' cost him his young life. I got his watch-key. I have had it, and that of another friend, in use for fifty years, and might say with truth that I never used them without thinking of the poor fellows.

Chapter Thirty
Orthes

On the 25th and 26th of February, our chief was examining Soult's position, which was a right good one as usual. It had the bend of a reaping-hook, and it was difficult for cavalry to approach from swamps and rocky ground. It was high ground above the 'Gave de Pau', and near to Orthes, where our friend Soult received battle. He had a fine army, and his best Generals commanding them, such as Drouet, Raille, Clausel, Villatte, Paris, Harispe, etc. There was a very handsome old bridge across the river at the town, fortified and mined. Above and below the bridge it was deep, and full of jagged rocks, and altogether a very formidable and dangerous place to run one's nose into without leave. There was some little fighting in the advance towards it, just to keep up the steam. We lost 20 or 30 men, but that went for nil. Early on the 27th the great row began. Wellington delivered battle (as old chroniclers used to say) to his warrior antagonist Marshal Soult, the favoured and favourite Lieutenant of the Emperor.

There were two valiant armies in the field, of some 40,000 men a side, besides cavalry and guns. Our approach to the French position on the heights was marshy and difficult, in some places our troops sinking up to their knees, and the enemy above pounding at them in the mire—painfully provoking. But still this only braced their nerves, and made them more savage. Just now there was more swearing than fighting, for this part of the force were struggling to get out of the mud, unable to use their arms. The cannonade and flashing of small-arms had now begun in earnest to echo down the river, through the town, and over the hills. All was in full play about nine o'clock, and continued all the day. The bold French rushed upon our columns with a wasting fire, and forced back our inferior numbers with unusually desperate valour, but our supports came up and shattered their masses. The nature of the ground would not permit very many to be engaged at this point; so that little progress was made, except in deadly slaughter, in which the French had the best of it.

Soult put all his reserves in motion, to complete what he supposed must be a victory all but gained, and 'twas said that he exclaimed aloud, 'I have him at last'. The moment, no doubt, was very dangerous, but Wellington's head was clear, and he had the most devoted hands and hearts to aid him, in the full assurance of another victory for old England. Amidst all this thundering din of battle, which shook the earth with violence, the Duke ordered Hill's division to ford the river on the French left, and get on their flank. It was deep to our loins. We slung the cartridge-boxes on top of the knapsacks, to keep our powder dry. The men linked arm in arm, to support each other in a very strong current.

Some cavalry formed in the river above us, to break the force of the stream. And so we all passed over unmolested, and marched on without halting for a moment, our shoes full of water, and our nether garments clinging to our bones, for none of us were very fat, but still in good working condition.

The 4th Division gained ground and secured a good position in the church and the graveyard (all ready for its victims). The French Marshal now rallied all his forces to make the grand coup that was 'at last to have him'. The thunder of the guns on both sides made the very hills quake. Our grand chief was wounded, with two other Generals, Ross and Walker. After fording the river, we drove back the troops there, seized the heights, cut off the French from the road to Pau, and turned the town of Orthes, menacing the only line of Soult's retreat. When his troops began to yield, our army advanced with an incessant and destructive fire of musketry and cannonade, losing men very fast, for the French saw their own danger, and fought like devils. But, seeing their retreat being cut off by Lord Hill, we hurried on until both sides began to run. They ran for dear life, and we kept to their heels, until coming up pretty close, down went their arms, after that their knapsacks.

They got into racing order in no time, and endeavoured to make good their escape. But our fellows got amongst a regiment with long greatcoats, and now Paddy Muldoon had fair play at last, as he said. I don't know haw many of these *parley-vous* he had caught by the tail, giving each of them a crack on the lug, as he termed it, pulling him down upon the sod, and telling him to stay there while he was hot after another, but never firing a shot at those unarmed.

Sir Stapleton Cotton with his cavalry got amongst them in another quarter, and cut them down by scores. Upwards of 2,000 threw down their arms, and their whole army now dispersed, *sauve qui peut*, leaving nearly 4,000 killed and wounded on the field of battle.

When the French broke, they made a rush for the bridge, which was soon choked up with baggage, broken gun-carriages, waggons, dead men and horses, thousands pressing forward to this point of escape. Our troops were in full pursuit, and cheering them on to destruction, while a brisk fire of artillery mixed up the living and the dead upon it. Our guns soon got the range, and kept it up, tearing to shatters every living thing attempting to escape that way. The skeletons of late strong fine regiments dashed into the boiling river on both sides, amongst the jagged rocks (peeping above the current), hoping thus to escape; but they only met another grave, nearly all perishing. It was an awful sight, as we passed that fine bridge, to see it covered with dead bodies and the debris of an army; the wounded groaning in torment, supplicating for water, and it so very near. The Duke was so hurt, he could not ride without pain, and so the pursuit was relaxed at sundown, when we gave up the chase, and then, weary enough and nothing in the larder, lay down on the sod, to dream of weeping and lamentation in England and France, our loss being 2,500 killed and wounded! *Cui bono?*

Chapter Thirty-One
Aire

After the affair at Orthes the medicos had great practice in carving. Maurice Quill was engaged with the French wounded a good deal, and while extracting a ball from the left side of an old veteran, he said, 'I hope you don't feel much pain.'

'Ah,' he said, in deep emotion, 'cut deeper, sir, and you will find the Emperor; he's buried in my heart!'

I was looking on while he was taking off the arm of another old soldier. When done, he laid hold of it, and tossed it up in the air, crying out '*Vive l'Empereur! Vive Napoleon!*' Such was the enthusiasm of those brave men.

The Duke of Richmond (then Lord March) had served on Lord Wellington's staff during the whole war without a scratch. He was a Captain in the 52nd Regiment, and, like a good and gallant soldier, joined his corps the night before the battle, to be shot through the body at the head of his company, thus learning by experience the difference between the labours and dangers of staff and regimental officers, which are in the inverse ratio to their promotions! We never got a step but by a death vacancy. The cold-hearted, ungenerous, self-interested arrogant directors of military affairs at home threw a wet blanket over young officers, unless there was a handle to one's name, court interest, or a hat-full of votes for a Tory minister!

What can ennoble knaves, or fools, or cowards?
Alas! not all the blood of all the Howards!

The Duke of Richmond was ever the friend of the old Peninsular army. He was a true and gallant soldier, brave and generous, and to him the remnant of the officers of that unconquerable army, so glorious to the arms of England, were indebted for the distinguished medal, bearing on clasps the names of numerous battles in which we were engaged. He represented the tardy justice to our Queen, the fourth crowned head for whom this army fought so many battles. And this noble and generous sovereign, best of all monarchs that ever filled an English throne, granted the request for all those victories achieved before she was born! The Duke of Richmond himself had ten clasps, and we gave him a splendid piece of plate to keep in continual family remembrance our love and respect for his manly and soldierlike bearing in behalf of the just claims of his comrades in war.

The battle of Orthes added another laurel to Wellington's name. It was another Sabbath-day's slaughter; somehow, most of our quarrels happened on Sunday, but I do not think that one in a hundred knew Saturday from Sunday, or Sunday from Monday, when in the field.

We followed up our friends the next day as close as we could, sticking to them like a burr to a sheep's tail. They made every effort to shake us off with a forced march and in light order, having left their arms behind them.

We had something to do as well in tinkering up our own broken ranks for the next scuffle, which was not far off. I believe, to do the thing well, an army ought to march twelve miles, fight a battle, and follow up the fugitives twelve miles farther to gain a great victory! I think we accomplished this more than once. It was surprising to find how soon the French troops rallied and made another stand after being dispersed and scattered like frightened sheep all over the country.

The weather was now very fine, which was always

cheery in the field, and we had some pleasant marching over *la belle France,* falling in at times with some of those domestic birds about barn doors and farmyards that will not get out of one's way. It was a serious matter to meddle with them or ruffle their feathers. A farmer did complain one day, after passing his gate, that he was minus a goose. A halt and a search was made, quite satisfactory to our honesty. But these gobblers make such a fuss when out of their own element, goosy was heard skirling and clapping her wings most violently, there was a tittering laugh amongst the men, and an oho! Another search-warrant, and the farmer's goose was discovered in a drum! A drumhead court-martial on the spot, and the drummer got goose without sauce for breaking the law, all the people about looking on in amazement with their mouths wide open at the severity and justice of our discipline in an enemy's country. Our military law was severe but necessary; hanging on to a tree for theft and violence was not uncommon, the dead bodies being left there for the vulture.

Lord Wellington's wound towards the end of the battle of Orthes saved the hostile army, and so they showed front again very soon at Aire. They always met us like lions; but in the end it was like hare-hunting. It may be that the French soldiers have a little more science in war than the soldiers of our country. The French look about them, and if they see their flanks being turned, or anything adverse to their forward movement, they consider it necessary to give way; while the ragged old red-coats always fought away right to their front, so long as they could see a Frenchman before them, leaving their officers to do the rest. This 'grand Wellington' of ours, as the Spaniards always talked of him, had a conception for arrangement and promptness never surpassed, decision and immediate action in all his preparations. The best Generals oftentimes grope in the dark, but Wellington's head was never under a cloud. He was a born soldier, while others were educated for the trade. It is one thing to fight a battle without fruits, another thing to fight a battle with success!

We came up with the enemy again on the 2nd of March, General Hill in command of our division as usual. We fell on them at once.

The action was sudden and severe, and was nearly lost to us at one moment when General Da Costa, a man of no ability, attacked with his corps of Portuguese in such a slovenly unsoldierlike way that he was repulsed and driven back in a charge by the French. As usual, we had to go to their aid. We had won the high grounds by this time, and spared two regiments, 34th and 39th to tinker up the damage. Our men got savage at the Portuguese for giving way, and I believe would have fired into them at the moment as heartily as into the French. With one vehement cheer, with one powerful charge, they went slap-dash into the enemy's columns, and drove them back on their reserves. But still they rallied, and renewed the battle with singular courage for fellows who had been whacked so often. But it was all in vain, the blood of the old bricks was up, and having now done so much, the whole division entered on the play, and with one great rush upon the poor French, General Harispe at their head, their ranks were broken, and we drove them into and right through the town of Aire.

They crossed the Adour, broke down the bridge, and made their way into the clouds of night, leaving us their dead to cover up. About 100 prisoners and a vast number of conscripts threw down their arms, and went away to their respective homes. They got very much into this practice when the army of France passed their doors, and was not likely to return that way.

They lost some valuable officers. Our General Barns was wounded, Colonel Hood killed, and some inferior officers, *i.e.* some Captains, Lieutenants, and Ensigns, small fry not worth talking of! It was not the fashion in those days to regard the death of a poor Subaltern more than that of a cavalry charger, yet many of the small fry lived to be great fishes. As to private soldiers, thousands upon thousands that joined the army from England were never heard of by their kindred or friends, dead or alive. They fought and they fell and were forgotten!

Before going into the town of Aire, I stepped into a house by the roadside to look for a drink of water, the day being very hot. The only tenant I could see was a very handsome young cavalry officer of ours, elegantly dressed, lying on his back and quite dead. He had been recently killed in an affair with French cavalry thereabouts by a shot from a rifleman. The fresh blood was oozing from a bullet-hole in his forehead, and, like so many of his brave comrades, he died facing the enemy. It was a charming day to spatter the early flowers of spring with human blood.

In sixteen days we had marched nearly one hundred miles, passed over five large rivers, forced the enemy before us, captured over 1,000 prisoners, six or seven guns, and magazines, and been everywhere victorious. Let us now have a little rest to patch up our duds. I got into a very respectable house, where the good dame had some knowledge of humanity, and must have seen a starvation-looking face every time she said to me *'Bon jour'*. I had not a franc in my pocket, and was too proud to ask for anything to eat. I had my rations, which did keep me alive, and one day a ham was sent into my room for my acceptance, which I finished off for breakfast, even polishing the bone. But I may as well explain that it was a goose ham well cured, smoked and bronzed, the first I had ever seen; but they are common in that part of the south of France.

The English army became popular in time. All the supplies were paid for in gold by us, while their own army did not respect property. It was said at the time that Soult remarked, 'I may expect to find by-and-by that the inhabitants will take up arms against us.'

I could see that the people rather liked the red-coats now, old prejudices were wearing out, our discipline was more perfect than the French, and everything was paid for. But there was no resting-place for the soles of our feet, and so we took leave of goose hams, and a quiet rest of a few days, to look after our fighting friends, and found them as usual well posted, and ready on this stage. A kind Frenchman brought me a large metal basin of water and a napkin to wash the dust out of my eyes. I thought the introduction very agreeable, and a preliminary of something for the interior department, as I fancied I smelt an omelet. The day was young, and the people here dined early. I had my horse put up and saw him fed, and now for a peaceful and a pleasant day, as I rubbed my hands with delight, when that in—1 bugle of ours, as all called it, joined in the naughty word, sounded the assemblee. There was no appeal against this music. There was a thundering cannonade going on not far distant, and so we were all out of the town in a crack, and killing each other in the usual way, *secundum artem*.

The French had been driven out of the town in the morning by the 95th Rifles, the most celebrated old fighting corps in the army, or perhaps in the world. They retired to their position to receive battle once more and try their luck, and bad luck attended them as usual, as Mother Skiddy predicted.

The action really now began, about twelve o'clock. Hill's artillery thundered away on the right, Clinton's on the left, Baron Alten attacked the centre. The French General, Harispe, was posted very strong on a hill, but was assailed most gallantly by some rifle battalions. The fight was brief and violent, a fiery combat, muzzle to muzzle. Of course our men would not give way, so the French did. Meantime we forced the passage of the river and sent Villatte and his troops away double quick. The country was now covered with confused masses of prisoners. Some tried to escape or hide themselves, others had thrown down their arms, crying out for quarter, while the wounded on both sides lay patient and still in all their agony.

This part of the country was flat, covered with vineyards, farm-houses, deep ditches, and inclosures, not at all suitable for cavalry. But our pursuit was stopped by General Clausell, who had four fresh divisions drawn up in our front right in our path, and all ready for battle. He lost no time in opening upon us all his batteries. However, it was now late, and night closed the scene upon all the combatants. Fighting for this day ceased, and in the morning the stage was clear, and not a Frenchman to be seen. We had lost a great many good soldiers, and a dozen valiant and most excellently brave officers. When the prison of the soul was broken up, the poor shattered shell lay there without burial, with no kindred friend to close the late brilliant eye, or say the last leave-taking words—*Requiescat in pace.*

I lay down under a fig-tree very tired with the day's excursion (my horse, of course, being in the rear, as usual on all fighting days) and disappointed of enjoying the hospitality ready for me at Tarbes.

We pushed on the next day after our beloved friends over the green hills of *la belle France*. Soult, we understood, was making for Toulouse, losing his young soldiers by the way; for, as soon as a conscript passed his home, he deserted. However, every bit of ground was disputed on our line of advance. Fighting was our daily bread, and I believe that officers and men went at it con amore, as they would follow a pack of harriers.

When we came up with their cavalry yesterday, old Major Doghearty, of the 13th Dragoons, might be seen charging at the head of his regiment, supported on his right and left by his two sons. Was not this a glorious sight of war and chivalry? Deeds of daring and of victory, too, bequeathed as an inheritance to the future armies of England. A new race of younger men soon stepped into their saddles and their shoes because they had no friends; no reward for the many and great achievements of this war. That terror of all tyrants, the press, had not the power, nor the pen, nor the freedom, nor the courage to speak out for the army as they have in the present day. So all heroic deeds were forgotten and left in abeyance, and clouds of darkness overshadowed the lives of hundreds of brave men who died in obscurity, many of them personally known to myself.

Our line of march was now directed on Toulouse, fighting our way and driving the rightful owners of the soil before us. A long wet day found myself and two messmates in a very comfortable and well-furnished chateau, of which we took possession for the night. The lawful owners having run away in alarm, the house now fell into the hands of three lads of different nations. We held a council of war how it was best to proceed with honour and justice. It was quite out of the question to starve in a cook-shop, or go without dinner in such fine quarters. A couple of old servants had been left in charge, so we thought it best, like gentle visitors, to ask them politely to prepare some supper for three Generals! *'O mon Dieu!'* they began both together, talking threescore to the dozen, keeping time with a jerking of the head, shoulders, arms and legs, in fact there was nothing in the house to eat or drink; but it was out of the question to take the word of an old French butler, so we began the evening's amusement in our way to forage. General Thomson and his servant took the outside of the dwelling, including the hen-roost; General Russell the interior; while General G. B. got up a good fire, collected feather-beds and blankets, and made a grand shake-down for three on the hearth of the library, where he lay in luxury awaiting the foraging party. By-and-by the two Generals and their staff appeared with a very good supply. The cook and butler got out of their alarm, and busied themselves, like good allies, in helping to prepare the evening meal. The library was a large room with a wide fire-place, and good enough for all we required. A couple of fowls were soon roasting before our fire, a flagon of wine on the table, and sausages, with a yard of bread! They made bread by the yard in this part of France, and sometimes in a ring as large as a horse-collar.

We all lay down by the fire now, quite cosy, our wet clothes hanging at the sides to dry, my little horse provided for. We were all as happy as three kings, when that bird of ill omen, our Adjutant, raised the latch and walked in, opened his roster-book, and warned me for outlying picket immediately!

'The men have fallen in and are waiting, please look sharp, sir. I thought I would not have found you out tonight.'

'Well, I'm very sorry you did find me, but you are always in luck finding me when you want an officer in a hurry for duty, besides, 'tis not my tour for picket tonight.'

'No, it is not,' he said, 'but Mr. W— can't be found, and you are next on the roster—you shall have an overslaw.'

No use battling with an old Adjutant like Peckett. Precise and correct in everything regarding his duty, he had been an excellent Sergeant-Major, and always gave the time to a second.

'What time is it, Peckett?'

'Ten minutes and a half past one, sir.'

He carried a load of a big silver watch as large as a turnip, which regulated the whole regiment!

Casting one glance at the fowls as they began to brown

at the fire, I turned out in the rain, and banged the door after me like thunder. I suppose I was in a thundering bad humour, but away I went in the dark about two miles with my good orderly men who never complained; reconnoitred the country as well as I could see, planted my sentries, and got the picket under cover in a brick-shed. There was a village in front, occupied by our cavalry. If I had been in my proper place, I ought to have been in advance of this village, but that was no business of mine. 'Obey orders', was the order of the day, and the night too.

I groped my way down to this cavalry quarter, called and requested to see General Long, in command of all the advanced posts here. He and his staff had just done dinner. I touched at once on the valour of his cavalry by saying, 'I am sent here, sir, to support you. My men are close by, what are your orders?'

'I don't require your aid at all,' he said, 'you may go back if you wish.'

'Very good, sir, I will return, for my men are wet and weary after a long day's march.'

'But you had better have some dinner before you go, 'tis getting late.'

I hesitated a moment, thought of home, and the pair of roast fowls and fireside! I declined the General's offer with all due thanks, made for my post, called in my sentries, and away we went quite jolly for our own quarters at a quick march.

All this took up as much time as would roast a sheep, but still I did not despond, but kept my eye on the mess dinner, in the luxurious hope of coming in for a bone. But, alas! when I got back, the two generals were asleep by the fireside where I left them, and the debris of the dinner on the table—some bones, a piece of bread, and the tail of a bottle of wine. I was horrified and called myself a stupid donkey, anything but an old soldier for not sitting down and eating my dinner at the table of a real General, when I had the blessed opportunity. I have not forgotten or forgiven myself yet, and thought—

Who fights to the end may win, but doubly wise,
Who knows the moment when to compromise,
And for a bird in hand, forbear to push
A doubtful search, for two inside the bush!

A ham and cold roast turkey just going from the General's table as I went in—dry bones, the tail of a sausage, a morsel of bread, and a driblet of wine was all I found on my return.

When dogs are hungry, they go to sleep—and so did G. B—!

Off again the next cock-crow, dodging our Gallic friends across the country. They roll people up in wet sheets in Germany, and put them to bed to make them warm. We are generally kept warm on the line of march, trudging along in our wet shirts, which dry on our bones when a blink of the sun favours us. We had got into a rainy week.

Chapter Thirty-Two
Marching Through France

Our General now crossed the Ariege river. Of course we never did pass a river, or could walk peaceably over a green sod in France, without being insulted by a shower of musket-balls, cannon-shot, or a dragoon sabre, ready to cut off a fellow's nose. *Vide* poor Captain C— of the Buffs, who lost his nose and an arm on the same day! Our dragoon sabres were sharp too, and left their mark behind them.

We were now approaching, at the beginning of April, the famous town of Toulouse, where Marshal Soult had pitched his tent, and hoisted his colours to make another stand, and another grand effort to beat Wellington. But six years of almost uninterrupted success had engrafted a seasoned, warlike strength and confidence into the very heart and muscles of our soldiers that made them invincible. They would willingly fall under their colours, and die in battle, but they would not be conquered at the eleventh hour, and so here was another pretty quarrel just going to begin.

My corps was distributed in some hamlets convenient to the river, where we kept watch, and kept ourselves warm for a few days, when the brilliant sun of France came forth to pay us a long visit, a most agreeable change which made us all very cheery. We had the big town before us; conjectures were innumerable; a thou sand opinions issued every day from all ranks.

Our baggage was up; commissariat supplies enough to feed the troops. We had wine, rations, and everything but money; still kept six months in arrear of our pay. But we knew that England was a good paymaster, and it would all come in a heap some day, if one lived to see it.

The river Garonne, as everyone knows, runs through Toulouse. The position was a valuable one for the French Marshal. A town, not regularly fortified, but made very formidable by batteries, redoubts, intrenchments, loop-holed houses, an ancient wall, the river, and a canal. All these places were ornamented with cannon, ready to salute the British General on his first appearance before the city. The suburb St. Cyprian was protected by an old wall, very thick, with towers and intrenchments, loop-holed houses, and batteries in the streets, all very nicely arranged to stop the progress of Lord Hill and his division. This was our allotment in the part of the play which was to come off very soon, in the teeth of General Reille and two divisions of the French army.

On the 27th of March our brigade was ordered up from Murat to get over a pontoon bridge at midnight. We found the river too wide for our number of boats, so gave that up. We tried it again on the 30th, when a new bridge was laid—crossed and recrossed, and yet that did not answer. I don't know why, I was not in the secret. It was a laborious work throwing over this bridge on a dark night. I was very tired! about two o'clock in the morning, the open door of a house which was close by invited me to look in; an old rickety straw bed, looking very lively, stood in the corner, upon which I lay down to have forty winks, positively no more, but was fast asleep in the crushing of a mosquito.

Unlawful slumbers are never refreshing; I had no business to be there. One is always jumping up and saying where am I? What brought me here? I opened my other eye (soldiers sleep, or ought to sleep, with one eye open), by the glimpse of a rushlight, and found myself hemmed in against the wall by our Brigadier-General, the Honourable

Sir Robert O'Callaghan, the biggest man in the whole division, snoring like a windmill.

'All right, little Bob (as he was sometimes called), if I have no business here, I'm sure you haven't, unless the pontoons are gone down with the stream. It is the first time I have had the honour of sharing a bed with any of the Lismore family. Bad luck to the fleas and all backbiters! Sleep on till I call you,' saying which I cautiously crept over the giant, to put my wet boot upon the face of another deserter, and to tumble over a third on the floor.

They both jumped up in alarm, and roused little Bob, who thought the French had him pinned up in a corner. I knocked over the glimmer for safety, leaving the trio in the dark to explain, if they wished, how they all got there while on duty!

I told this little anecdote to the dear old General long afterwards at one of his dinner parties at Madras, when he was there as Commander-in-Chief, which made him laugh heartily, and introduced many of the old stories and anecdotes of the Peninsula—not in an old tent, but in a splendid palace. He was a brave soldier, and a powerful Irishman. He carried a big sword, and used it at times with great effect, slashing the heads of Frenchmen in the 'Donnybrook Fair' style. He would cut them down right and left, and upon one occasion, when his sword was shattered in his hand, he got hold of a big shillelagh, and laid about him like a thresher with a flail, and never afterward gave it up; it answered so well, he said. But like the rest of the gallant band, he dropped into his narrow cell, and was soon forgotten.

There were many ways of meeting the enemy in combat, but who ever heard of an officer going into battle with a pocket full of stones? It was a sort of pastime with a Captain Irvine, of the old 'Slashers'. He was a capital shot with a stone, and a very strong, able, active man, left-handed, who delivered his shot with such force and accuracy that he would knock a fellow into next week. He never minded meeting two or sometimes three Frenchmen, when they were detached. Pretty sure of knocking one down with a stone, he sprang upon the other like a leopard, and knocked him on the head with his own firelock, and with one great, thrilling shout he paralyzed the third. If he did not trip him up he frightened him out of reach, pelting him with stones as he ran. All this gymnastic play created at times roars of laughter amongst the men, for it never was done in a corner, nor for bravado. This brave Irish gentleman and soldier survived the war, but never reached any rank beyond a Captain.

Chapter Thirty-Three
The Battle of Toulouse

Our men began to fix their flints and examine their powder on the 9th as we approached the town, and took up our quarters in front of St. Cyprian. The weather was fine, everyone jolly, and the Patlanders in particular cracking their jokes. 'How the d---l are we to get over that big sthrame av a river to leather them vaga-bones out o' that?' says Paddy Muldoon, for he wasn't kilt yet.

'O, niver mind,' says another old cripple, who lost an eye on the Nive, 'that countryman av yours wid the long nose will show you the way when he's riddy.'

'O, be gar, then, we'll not wait very long, for I seen him over here this morn wid our Farmer Hill, spying them wid his long eye-glass, an' he won't keep us waiting. But there's oceans on 'em down there in the town pickin' holes in the wall, and fencen all the houses, so mind that other eye av yours!'

They were ever laughing and cracking their Irish jokes at the worst of times.

The Duke crossed the river about fourteen miles below the town, on his pontoon bridge, with the Light Division; and early in the morning he formed his army. On Easter Sunday morning, the 10th of April 1814, I was very comfortably seated in the library of a chateau belonging to some stupid fellow who had run away in alarm, leaving his hall door open. We were preparing a breakfast of fresh eggs and bacon, which were quarrelling in the frying-pan outside in the sunshine, when bang! went the signal-gun, and Freeman, our trusty bugleman, sounded the assemblee at once. Whilst the men were getting on their packs and their arms ready, we gobbled up the contents of the frying-pan, left our traps in charge of servants, fell into our places, and marched down to join in the bloody fray of another Sabbath day's unholy work. It was very handy for us, not far to go, and all fresh as young colts. In twenty minutes we came to the scratch, and were hard at work fighting in the town. On the suburbs on the left bank of the river, where the enemy had two divisions under the command of Count Reille. It is always ugly, dangerous work fighting in a town; so many holes and corners, hiding-places and loop-holes, where one may be picked off by an unseen enemy. This was just our case, fighting from house to house and from street to street, our men having their bones cracked, and dropping off at every corner. As the enemy retired, or were driven back, they fired the houses they left, to arrest our progress, not sparing their own property. We found in many houses the furniture piled up in rooms, ready for the torch. The streets were barricaded, and cannon planted at every entrance, pounding away at the first blink of any red-coat. But our men dashed on through fire and smoke, and carried on the work surely and gradually, for we lost nothing that we gained. Our senior Captain Baker, had that morning got his majority, and was one of the first killed. He had come all the way from India to join our battalion. Other officers had been with the regiment in all its battles, and had never been hit five years—such is the fate of war!

There was a furious row going on across, the river, a tremendous crash of great guns and small-arms. The two Marshals had met, with their two valiant armies, and quarrelled. They were always fighting and quarrelling. Saturday or Sunday was all the same to them, and here they were at it on an Easter Day, a festival of solemnity in all

Christian lands, but not the least regarded on the banks of the Garonne. The battle went on with desperate fury, both sides determined to win the fight. It was a charming day, and worthy of better deeds than destroying life. We had the bravest, the best, the finest-disciplined and well-seasoned army in the world; fighting was their daily bread—it gave them an appetite. No other soldiers on earth had a chance against them in fair and open ground. The Duke knew it, and let them loose this morning.

There was pounding on both sides of the river in full force about noon, the French having all the advantage. Their two miles of position along Mont Rave were defended by intrenchments, breastworks, redoubts, and immense batteries bristling with cannon. Our side, too, looked as formidable. I never had, personally, any taste for fighting in the dark, or in the streets, although we used to practise the art of 'street-firing and retiring'. All fudge!

The advance towards the French position was very swampy and unfit for cavalry or the passage of guns. This alone would shake the nerves of any other man than Wellington, but, always confident, he relied on his own British soldiers.

General Freyve, a Spanish leader, asked permission to have the honour of leading his troops first into battle. Granted—and away they went, 9,000 strong, with a good reserve, very resolved to have all the victory to themselves. The French began to torment them, as they advanced, with a shower of lead. They wavered, and rushed for shelter into a deep hollow. The French, now taking the advantage of war, turned out of their breastworks and poured volley after volley into the poor Spaniards, the bullets hissing through their quivering flesh as hard as they could tear, the enemy at their heels, until too near our cavalry, mortifying to the Duke, but the only remark he made was—

'Well, I have seen some curious sights, but I never saw

10,000 men running a race before!'

Sir Thomas Picton failed in his attack at another point, entirely from disobeying his master's orders; turning a false attack into a real one, and losing thereby his chance of success, and 400 men and officers. Poor Sir Thomas never could bridle his ardour when he had a chance of a dash at the French. But dashing in war means courage without prudence.

We had now forced the first line of intrenchments and barricades on our side. The second we looked at, but it had such a very angry appearance that we slackened our fire to bide our time and listen to the music on the other side. The crisis was approaching with some good promise to the French, the Spaniards being utterly routed. General Picton had been repulsed, and our men, frightfully reduced in numbers, were making their way to the French position through a deep swamp tangled with many other obstacles, a heavy fire of great guns and musketry being poured into their teeth the whole way, they not returning a single shot. What other troops in the world would have faced such a storm of death? But they did advance, and met Taupin's whole force rushing down upon them. At this moment some rockets were discharged from our side, got amongst the Frenchmen's legs with an unheard-of hissing, curving, serpentining, biting, and kicking noise that they never saw or heard before. It staggered their courage and steadiness long enough to let General Lambert's brigade make a rush with a cheer amongst them, with such irresistible power that they went to the right-about and fled. Taupin was killed, and our people gained the platform.

Soult, seeing this danger, brought up all his artillery to make a clearance of this little force, aided by double numbers of infantry. But the domineering courage of British soldiers overcame this obstacle, and decided the first act of the play. The Scotch Brigade and the Portuguese, with

Marshal Beresford's division, dashed on next, scrambling up the hill; all the breastworks and batteries in their front pouring a wasting fire into their face, did not stagger their courage. The French yielded here for a little, but rallied and returned with their reserves, and there was an awful struggle. General Harispe encouraged his men, and fought with them with great vigour. He surrounded the redoubts we had taken, and broke in upon the 42nd Highlanders. This gallant corps fought so bravely against such long odds that there were but few blue bonnets left in half an hour. The fighting was desperate here. Our men fell fast and were soon reduced to a 'thin red line' of old bricks. The French had the advantage from numbers and position, but the British, regardless of numbers at any time, go in to win. Harispe and another General had now fallen, fighting like game-cocks. Our 6th Division rushed on madly for a victory, and kept the ground until the French left the platform. Soult, seeing that the red-coats had won the day, abandoned the field, covered with slain, relinquished the whole of Mont Rave, further resistance being useless, and retired into Toulouse.

This was what I would call honest good fighting, face to face, hand to hand on the open field, the usual practice in the Peninsula. On the other side we had gained a good many streets, and kept them. Wherever a head appeared from under cover it was in danger of being cracked with a dozen bullets. I had myself some providential escapes. Passing into a long, narrow, shady street, very quiet, and no one visible, a cannon-shot came whistling past my head so close I felt the wind of the ball on my cheek, which whift me round. I darted into a house in a jiffy, when another came bang after me, passed through the room, and fell from the opposite wall.

My Captain had just turned the same corner, when I warned him to look out, and only just in time to save his life, for which he blew me up, saying, 'You never keep your eyes open, or you might have seen that gunner at the top of the street just waiting to crack your wild head.'

I peeped out at the door, and, sure enough, there he was, standing by his gun, ready to blow the match. I rolled his own shot out into the street, keeping my eye on him, but he fired no more.

One of our men saw him, and 'made him lave that sure,' as he said, for 'I saw him fire on the Captain, and only waited to creep near enough to pitch him over!'

Curious to see how the battle was going on over the river, I invited our Colonel, Worsley, to accompany me for a *belle-vue* quite at hand.

'Where are you going to take me?' he said, 'remember every house is full of sharpshooters, and if I follow you, it will surely be into their company.'

'Oh no, 'tis all safe. I have got a ladder here, we will top this house and see a bit of the fight on the other side. Did you ever hear a more terrific fire?'

By this time we had clambered up to the top of a house, keeping a big brick chimney in our front, just high enough to look over to see some of the murder over the way, but had not long enjoyed the view when the brick-dust was knocked out of the chimney by a shower of bullets, we not having calculated that our heads were not only visible, but the very shell of humanity exposed to be cracked like an egg.

When the ostrich is pressed hard in the chase he runs his head into a bush or into the sand, and considers himself safe! I don't think we much exceeded the wisdom of this stupid bird upon this occasion of our curiosity. The next volley, which came fast sent us away double quick rolling down, ladder and all, and nearly broke our necks. I got off cheap enough with a slight wound; Colonel Worsley had his epaulet spoiled with a shot, and a ventilator made in his shako.

We kept pounding away until night drew the curtain over a wide scene of painful misery. Multitudes of wounded lay scattered over miles of ground; the agony and torment and shrieks and helpless condition of thousands found no relief for a long time. Hundreds died in the night for want of care, for it was impossible for the medicos to attend to half the wounded. The living had a heavy day of fatigue and fighting with great excitement, but their hands and their hearts were up to their work, in spite, of any reaction.

The programme of the Easter Sunday was now closed. The men lighted the camp-fires and sat round them cooking and chatting over the ration dinner and absent comrades.

Next day was a *dies non*, i.e. we had no fighting worth talking of. We kept all the town we gained, and the French kept the rest. We buried the dead in shallow graves. Both parties kept a sharp look-out on each other all day. I went on outlying picket at night with instructions to be wide awake, and feel my way at the dawn of day towards the bridge if I met with no opposition.

On the morning of the 12th, at grey dawn, I was feeling my way with the picket without opposition. Arriving at the fine stone bridge, I found it barricaded all the way over with hogsheads filled with earth and stones and gravel. Walking over these, I came to the ponderous iron gate, locked and fastened with heavy chains. When the people saw me advance with my party of red-coats, they came down with goodwill, with crowbars, and forced the gate open, arid gave us a cheer and a welcome, so that I had the honour of being the first British officer that entered Toulouse. Here I halted until my own corps came up. We then marched in, colours flying, drums beating, all very jolly, and halted for an hour in the street waiting for orders. In the meantime most of the officers popped into a cafe to get some breakfast. The windows and balconies were soon crowded with ladies, waving their white kerchiefs, and throwing down amongst us bouquets of fresh flowers, as if they had sprung up spontaneously. The white cockade appeared as if by magic everywhere, although the French army had not been out of the town twelve hours.

We fancied that we were now to be left here in this garden of Eden amongst sweet flowers and pretty girls that were smiling down upon our tattered red coats—vain imagination!

An atrocious cocked hat of an aide-de-camp came riding up with a smirk, saying, 'Colonel Worsley, you are to follow up the enemy on the Toulon road with your regiment as quickly as you can. You will receive subsequent orders'; and away he went, after destroying all our hopes and pleasant waking dreams.

I believe our fighting Colonel was the only one who wished to advance in such a hurry, and not to retard our progress a moment, he paid the breakfast at the cafe and hurried us off.

Chapter Thirty-Four
Napoleon Abdicates

The whole French army had taken to their heels in the night and filed through the town. As they passed on they broke down the bridges over the canal to impede our line of march. But we never came up with them again, nor smelt the perfume of tobacco and onions which tainted the air behind them. We halted at the little town of Villefranche, and there we heard by an express from Paris that Napoleon the Grand had abdicated, and that the Allies were in the capital of *la belle France*, and all the rest of it. This was all very serene, and I believe joyful news to most of us, for in reality we had enough fighting and marching and starving for a long time to come. At all events I thought so, and was quite content with the little share and small part I had in the campaign, having marched through Portugal, all over Spain, and well into France. I had been in thirteen engagements with the next best troops in the world, and escaped for three years out of the hands of the Philistines without any broken bones, a providential and rare occurrence in those days, when one considers the rough usages of war, and that we left in Spain and France the bones of nearly 100,000 men; most of them bleaching in the sun, after being picked bare by the vulture and the wolf.

We now considered the war at an end, and began to enjoy ourselves in a fashion, proud of our conquests and the glory of our arms, a stirring sound amongst all ranks. But war is never far away. From man to the very smallest insect, all are at strife.

After conquest one begins to count the cost. War is a great evil, and a very expensive trade. In this one England expended more than a hundred millions sterling money on her own operations, besides an immense expenditure on Spain and Portugal. Her land forces fought and won eighteen pitched battles, besides affaires and combats without number, took four great fortresses by siege, and sustained ten others. Two hundred thousand of the enemy were killed, wounded, and prisoners.

It was said the Duke of Wellington committed faults. Who ever heard or read of a great commander making war in all things faultless? He was a great general, with a patient foresight, a clear judgment, prompt and decisive, insuring the whole confidence of his army, and yet had to contend against the Governments of England, Spain, and Portugal; all retarding his progress and casting dust in his eyes. All those to whom he looked for support were jealous and vindictive, even the Cabinet Ministers of his own country. And they say he committed faults—what were they? England had no army until he made one. He landed in Portugal with 9,000 men, and beat back the armies of France to their own firesides. He had rare qualities as a commander. He overthrew the great conqueror Napoleon, the swell and dash of a mighty wave, before whom kingdoms fell. If you fight for England you should always win, and what English General was ever so victorious as Wellington?

In summing up accounts and returns for the last few days, it appeared that we had lost 4 Generals and 4,659 officers and men, killed and wounded. Total loss of the French, 5 Generals and 3,000 officers and men, ditto; a useless and lamentable sacrifice of life, Napoleon having abdicated before the battle. A Colonel Cook and a French Colonel, St. Simon, had been despatched from Paris to make known to the two armies that hostilities must now cease. These officers were detained on the road by the police, near Blois, where the Empress Louisa was holding a court. This officious detention cost the blood of 7,000 brave men, which flowed over Mont Rave and through the streets of Toulouse.

My regiment returned to the gay city of Toulouse, where we were quartered. The officers were billeted here and there through the town. 'Tis all a lottery; one may get into an hospitable house, another may find a vinegar-face of a landlady. I was not over lucky, but my room was clean, and I lived as best I could on my promissory note, the six months' pay due, the great sum of about £55, deducting income tax, which was levied from the pay of the junior Ensign!

The Duke of Wellington established his headquarters in Toulouse. There was no end to gaiety. We were out at balls, concerts, and evening parties. We had the *entree* into all the theatres to any part of the house for a franc. The people seemed happy and rejoiced over the new order of things. The town had not suffered in the least during the killing and slaying outside, excepting on our side of the river, which was plundered, fired, and demolished by the French troops as they were beaten back. The Duke did not suffer a shot or shell to be thrown into the city when held by the vanquished troops after their retreat from Mont Rave, and of course gained the respect and esteem of the citizens for his consideration and humanity.

The Duke d'Angouleme made his public *entree* into the city escorted by Wellington and his staff, and all the dignitaries of the town and country. I went out with the rest of the cocked hats and feathers to meet him some distance off, being well mounted on a spunky horse, who would be in the front. He carried me, *nolens, volens*, alongside of the Royal Duke, when and where I was admonished by Sir E. P--, and ordered to fall back! I never had a very thin skin, and did not torment myself at this checkmate. But I have known an officer who was so hurt by receiving a rebuke at the head of his regiment that he went deranged, was placed in an asylum, and never recovered. He was a most excellent officer, and had his regiment in first-rate order, until he met this uncouth savage of an Inspecting-General.

The Duke's welcome home was echoed everywhere by old and young. Fresh and fair, aged men in heads of snow, all pressed forward to kiss his stirrup.

After six weeks of refreshing jollification, we got the route for Bordeaux. I was glad of the expected change of quarters; we had a few days' notice to quit, and lighten our baggage. I sold my three horses to raise the wind and pay my debts. I did not realise for the three so many dollars as one of them had cost me, the market being overstocked with horses, mules, and donkeys, all at a fearful discount, every officer selling off. I was not very well at this time. I suppose a regular kind of life and a feather-bed did not agree with my former manner of life on the green sod. Our doctor recommended me to go down the river with the invalids in an open boat. Barges were provided for the sick and wounded soldiers, small boats for small parties of officers. The weather being charming, we required neither sails nor oars, so away we went, smoothly gliding over the silver stream, one man steering (it was hard work for the poor horses pulling up those heavy barges against the stream).

We landed every evening at some village on the banks of the fine river to pass the night. The dames from the different *auberges* made a rapid descent upon us the moment we landed, with such a clatter and noisy invitation to go their respective houses—every thing so nice, so good, superior, and such moderate terms. They were abusing each other all the time in the most distingue fashion. We knew pretty well what was meant by moderate terms, all that they could screw out of famished pockets. After exhausting all their polite language, if it is possible to tire a Frenchwoman's tongue, we took a peep into their respective shells, selected our lodgings, and made our bargain. This was a necessary arrangement in France, and all over the Continent, to prevent disputes, over charges, and imposition.

However, they bustled about with good humour, and made us all so very comfortable, that we would have remained there willingly for weeks if we could. The situation was so charming, so peaceful; no parades nor drills, nor a chance of one's bones being broken with shot or shell. How wonderful was the feeling of quiet; no trampling of horses, nor clashing of arms, nor "*tir-whit*" of a shell, or the whop of a cannon-ball, splashing the mud in one's face, or perhaps the brains of your *camarado*.

Three delightful days we passed on the Garonne, and then brought up in the beautiful town of Bordeaux, amongst fruit and flowers, choice wine, and nice friendly people. The first stage, homeward bound—it all appeared as a holy dream. Our last run down was a short one. On landing, four of us went to a cafe and ordered breakfast—a good one, and no mistake. We were hungry as hunters, and were well served. We cast lots who was to pay the bill. I was the Jonas, and it just cleared me out to a cent, and left me in every sense in light marching order. Not a penny at my command—let loose in a large city, full of luxury, frolic, and fun, I searched all my pockets in vain for a single franc to get a scrubby dinner, but it was no go; so I went in search of my billet. After roving about the city for some hours, I found No. 2 Rue St. Colomb—Monsieur Ducasse—knocked at the door and presented my ticket to the servant, who took it up for examination. After surveying me with wonder or admiration, never having seen a red-coat at No. 2 before, I was received kindly, and shown upstairs to a suitable room, for sitting and sleeping in combined, and left there to look out at the window, to turn over in my mind how or where I was to find my servant and my baggage, which was reduced into so small a compass that he could easily carry it on the top of his knap-sack, along with firelock and the rest of his war tools, for I had discarded the frying-pan and all the other camp toggery. I made a start into the town, without money or credit—nothing but an alarming appetite. I knew I had my rations to fall back upon, but I could not find my servant, nor could he find me—we were both lost. I rambled about in search of him for hours, and did not find No. 2 till late, when I was presented with some light supper of salad or vegetable diet. A round of boiled beef would have been more in my way, but I never saw one in France.

The kind landlord now told me that I must never be out of the way at three o'clock—it was their dining hour. I must always breakfast and dine with the family, and be one of themselves while I remained, or he would be very angry, with an emphasis on the word and a smile on his honest face—a friendly offer which I accepted with thanks. Particularly lucky I thought myself, as there was nothing in my department but the rations and a thundering appetite. I had permission to draw my rations once a week in a heap, which was sent to the kitchen of my landlord. The next morning I made my debut at the breakfast table, after waiting about three hours beyond my usual time. An early tasse of *cafe noir* keeps a Frenchman alive until the *dejeuner* at eleven o'clock. I was introduced to Madame and the fair Clementine, not out of her teens, and the son, an agreeable young fellow, who spoke English "a leetle." We became great allies and correspondents for many years afterwards. I found my stray cook and butler, who was also a guest and lived in clover—nothing to do but clean my boots and study French in the cuisine. His name was Death, which may account for many escapes in battle, he being the destroyer never to be destroyed; but he was a stupid fellow at any foreign language! The young lady played on the harp and piano, and was really an accomplished, pretty, bashful girl, who was sent to Mass very often with her maid, and to confess her sins to a crafty old priest who might have excused her innocence. The absolution was required within the box, not from the simple child on its knees outside.

They had little music parties of an evening. On one of those occasions a French officer came up to me and looked at my buttons, being, as he said, familiar with the No. 34, and asked me if there was an officer named Day in the regiment, and if I knew anything of him.

'Oh, yes! he was our Adjutant, but was unfortunately killed on the Pyrenees on the 25th of July last, when you paid us that most unfriendly visit.'

'Not so,' he said, 'but was mortally wounded. I found him on the battlefield after he had been plundered, and spoke to him. He gave me the sign and token of a brother of our craft, and, being a Freemason myself, I took him from that moment under my charge. I was sent to Bayonne with our wounded and many of your prisoners. Poor Day was my especial care—I got him so far, and made his wasting life as quiet to him as possible. He wanted for many things that I had not in my power to provide. I got him cash for a bill on England, which I may say was duly honoured, but he did survive over a couple of weeks or so, and was buried with Masonic honours.'

This was the finale of a good soldier. He fell into the kind hands of a brother Mason, and was not left, as we thought, on the field amongst the slain, to be devoured by the vultures. I resolved, after hearing this little chivalric story, to become a Freemason if I got safe home, and I kept my word. The Brethren are to be found amongst all nations; and if you can make yourself known, you may be sure of aid, friendship, and security. Although denounced by the Pope as heretics and out of the pale of the Church, I can assure his Holiness they are the most loyal of her Majesty's subjects, staunch supporters of her Crown and dignity, and of the Church of England as established by law, and on this subject the opinion of the Pope is worthless beyond the Vatican.

Our army was now encamped about seven miles from Bordeaux. As if we had not fighting enough, certain regiments were selected to embark for America, to begin a new war with people who could speak English. Our wise law-makers at home were too fond of settling disputes in those days with powder and lead. The expedition embarked for New Orleans under the command of Lieutenant-General Sir Edward Pakenham, brother-in-law to the Duke of Wellington, an able and gallant officer who passed through the Peninsular war to be killed by an American rifleman from behind a bale of cotton.

Chapter Thirty-Five
The End of the Campaign

The rest of our army began to embark for England as ships arrived. In the meantime there was much unpleasant work and bad feeling between French and English officers. Both were so habituated to fighting it seemed quite out of their power to give it up—like two game-cocks who meet on the same path, they must have a kick at each other! There was a feeling of deep jealousy against us; we received much attention, and the ladies favoured the British officers with smiles, which made things worse. There were many quarrels, and the *Duello* came into practice. The theatres were crowded, and some of our officers were insulted one night by their antagonists. To insult one red-coat then was an insult to all, and so there was a general row, the French officers being driven out of the house. The next night there was a great muster of both parties, I believe for the purpose of renewing the war or opening a new campaign at Bordeaux. The Frenchmen had their swords, the English officers none. The Irish gentlemen carried shillelaghs, as they do at Ballymacrack, in Tipperary. Somehow a nice little quarrel was soon got up about some ladies who were receiving attention from the boys of Kilkenny, every one of them nearly six feet high. Indeed, the sweet girls of Kilkenny, although not so tall, are very fine specimens of Divine art—so fair and so fresh—

> *Their cheeks are like roses,*
> *Their lips just the same,*
> *Or like a dish of ripe strawberries*
> *Smothered in cream.*

The French ladies not appearing to countenance any but those big Irishmen, sharp words were spoken against all red-coats, a great many frowns. Swords were half unsheathed and dashed back into the metal scabbard with a sort of clang of defiance—the blood of St. Patrick was roused. Those gentle creatures, whose trade was killing and slaying, did not require much fuel to get up their steam. One of the Fitzgerald's 'Light Division', a battering-ram of himself, drew his stick half-way up through his left hand, and sent in down again with a bang on the floor, looking pistols and daggers. There were some sarcastic words, then a shove and a scuffle, which soon increased to something like an Irish row at Donnybrook Fair, when the Frenchmen were banged out of the theatre wholesale. All this play began in the lobby between the acts, and, as the last of the blue-coats went rolling down the stairs, some one above cried out, '*Exeunt omnes!*' and all was quiet. Next morning was fixed for the Duello, the general finale of such sports. Blood was spilt on both sides very freely, and one or two gentlemen were qualified for a wake. Preparations were being made for a great fighting field-day on the following morning, but the whole of last night's campaign being reported to our Commander-in-Chief, hostilities were suspended by a general order. All officers were prohibited going again to this theatre, under certain pains and penalties.

The French officers were ordered by their chiefs to retire across the Garonne to their own quarters.

In defiance of the general order, some of our officers had the imprudence to return to the same theatre, but found a sergeant there with a book to insert the name of any who insisted on going in. With one exception they all retired, and that exception was the senior Captain of my own regiment, an old officer who ought to have shown a better example. When the book was sent next morning to the

Adjutant-General, Captain B— was placed in arrest, and had his choice to stand a court-martial or quit the service. He chose the latter, and gave a step in the corps, a most unfortunate finale and deeply regretted by all his friends. But the first duty of the British soldier is to obey orders!

My regiment lay in camp some miles from the city. I was too comfortable myself with my kind friends at No. 2 to mix in any of these broils. Their hours were early, and the family quiet and happy, nor was it my part to be out late, so I stayed at home. The good landlord used to say to me every day at dinner, 'No ros-beff, Monsieur George', and the kind lady always gave me Benjamin's portion at breakfast *a la fourchette*!

My corps had nothing to do, so they did not want me, nor was I at all anxious to leave my town residence.

I went out one day to pay them a visit, and to see Sir Lowry Cole on a little private affair. General Cole was a neighbour of ours when at home, and always ready to do me a service, but we seldom met. He commanded the 4th Division of the army. On this occasion he got me leave of absence to precede my regiment going home. My turn for leave was far distant, so I came the old soldier over my seniors. But they forgave me after much chaffing, such as 'We suppose that General Cole is going to take you on his personal staff, and, of course, you must go home for your cocked hat and feather.'

'O, no doubt, old fellow, lucky enough for the man who has a home to go to. I will be happy to see you all at my chateau when your time comes to be quartered in our country town.'

And the time did come in reality, and the officers, one and all, were welcome guests at Belle-vue when I was far away, frying in the East Indies, in another campaign, and in another regiment.

But here I am, still passing a day at the camp near

Bordeaux hearing all the news, seeing all my old comrades, the men of my company, and everyone, as if I had been absent a year, everybody jolly, oceans of money, and no end to good living for man and horse! An issue of six months' back pay in gold opened the eyes, and the mouths, and the hands, and the hearts of a whole army. The matter was how to spend it. Soldiers like sailors win their money like horses, and spend it like asses. There was no lack of wine-houses and restaurants, dominoes, pitch and toss: Head, I win!—tail, you lose!—anything to catch the penny. So their thirty or forty dollars did not last long.

'What about our old friend, Mrs. Commissary-General Skiddy?' I asked one of my sergeants.

'O, be gad, sir, she's all right and fresh as a chamrog. There she is, sir, crossing the green, would you like to speak to her?'

'Yes, I will hail her myself. Hiloo, mother Skiddy, come over here till I look at you, and see if it's yourself or your ghost?'

'Oh then, Musha, God bless you my dear, sure it's myself that's glad to see your honour alive, after being kilt on the top of a house in the great battle when I was away in the care of Dan. Sure they reported down where I was, you were kilt entirely. But, my legs, it's right well you're looking, the Lord Presarve ye, and sure Dan was so sorry for yer honour, and said, "how many's the mile you carried his firelock for him on the long march", for he was sometimes bent, tired, and ready to dhrop. An ye know, sir, when I found him smashed up in that battle at Saint Peter's, he says to me, "Biddy," says he, "I'll never march any more, for my leg's bruck in two heves, by that pagan that kilt me." Well, sir, when the doctor cum to set his leg, it wasn't bruck at all, only a big hole in it, but 'twas mighty sore; an sure I have him here now as good as new. All the men as was wounded, barrin' the killed, cum up here t'other day. Would you like to see Dan, sir?'

'Surely I must see him before I go home—I'm going to Ireland soon.'

'Is it to ould Ireland, sir? sure that's me own counthry, the blessin' av all the saints be wid yer honour, sure it makes me heart bounce when I think av being there agin.' And wiping her eye with a corner of her very white apron, she ran away for Dan.

He was a very wiry piece of stuff, not over five feet three, but able to do more work than two lanky fellows all backbone and no muscle. He was always at his post, and a great enemy to them vagabones, the French!

'Well, Dan Skiddy, I'm glad to see you looking so fresh after being killed at Saint Pierre in that big fight. You will soon be qualified for the pension, and we hope you'll get the shilling.'

'O, then good luck to yer honour, and sure it's yourself that would make it fifteen pence if ye cud, for I marched a power in Spain, and kilt a good dale av the French, bad scram to them the vagabones.'

'O Dan, avourneen, don't be cursin' the Frinch now that we're done wid 'em; sure they couldn't help it, the crathers, bein' paid to fight for ould Bony himself.'

'Well, you know how they murdered my leg, Biddy.'

'Sure that's their naither, dear, to murder every one av us, but the pace has made them quiet and civil now. O, me back!'

'What's the matter with your back, Biddy?'

'O, yer honour knows how my back was bruck on the rethreat from Madrid down to Portugal in the short days of winter rains, when everybody was lost. But Dan made promise niver to tell any one, and there he is forenenst me,' giving him a sly look for permission to tell her story.

'Yer honour minds how we were all kilt and destroyed on the long march last winter, and the French at our heels, an' all our men droppin' and dyin' on the roadside, waitin' to be killed over agin by them vagabones comin' after us. Well, I don't know if you seed him, sir, but down drops poor Dan, to be murdered like all the rest. Says he, "Biddy dear, I can't go on furder one yard to save me life." "O, Dan jewel," sis I, "I'll help you on a bit; tak' a hould av me, an' throw away your knapsack." "I'll niver part wid my knapsack," says he, "nor my firelock, while I'm a soger." "Dogs then," sis I, "you 'ont live long, for the French are comin' up quick upon us." Thinkin', ye see, sir, to give him sperret to move, but the poor crather hadn't power to stir a lim.

'Now I heerd the firin' behind, and saw them killin' Dan, as if it was! So I draws him up on the bank and coaxed him to get on me back, for, sis I, "the French will have ye in half an hour, an' me too, the pagans." In truth I was just thinkin' they had hould av us both, when I draws him up on me back, knapsack an' all. "Throw away your gun," sis I. "I won't," says he. "Biddy, I'll shoot the first vaga-bone lays hould av your tail," says he. He was always a conthrary crather when any one invaded his firelock.

'Well, sir, I went away wid him on me back, knapsack, firelock, and all, as strong as Sampson, for the fear I was in. An' fegs, I carried him half a league after the regiment into the bivwack. Me back was bruck entirely from that time to this, an' it'll never get strait till I go to the Holy Well in Ireland, and have Father McShane's blessin', an' his hand laid over me! An' that's all the thruth, yer honour, I've told ye.'

'Well, Mrs. Skiddy, you are a wonderful little woman. You saved a good soldier for yourself and the service. All the regiment knows how well you acted on the march, where we lost so many of our gallant comrades. You have been always a most useful person, well respected, and I wish you safe home to the Green Isle, and a safe meeting with your friends and Father McShane! But where was your donkey all this time?'

'Och then, yer honour knows when that murderin' villain shot our poor donkeys. I helped on the back of my wee fellow all that he could carry, to save what I could for the poor women whose dead beasts were left on the roadside. So I was left to walk myself, and carry poor Dan a bit. The curse av the crows be on his fire-finger that shot the donkeys.'

I bid this wonderful structure of humanity a friendly farewell, after squaring a long account with her for about a year's washing and darning. She was reluctant to take anything, saying, 'O, sir, sure you always belonged to me own company, an' you're welcome to the bit av washing.'

I hope Dan got the shilling, i.e. a shilling a day pension for life.

But the Government of the day that wasted with unsparing hand England's gold in millions, passed off with a sixpenny pension the old soldier, bearing many scars, and very often with sixpence or ninepence a day for nine, twelve, eighteen, or twenty-four months, when it ceased and he became a pauper.

The sinecures held in those days by the aristocracy and their friends and relations for doing nothing would have pensioned for life thousands of brave men who fought nobly for their country and their king.

But the war was now over, and as the historian, the great and gallant good Napier, said in his conclusion, 'Thus the war terminated, and with it all remembrance of its veterans' services'.

If you enjoyed 'Ensign Bell of the Cumberland Gentlemen' you may also enjoy other books set in the Peninsula published by Leonaur.

These include:

Rifleman Costello
by Edward Costello

Captain of the 95th (Rifles)
by Jonathan Leach

Napoleonic War Stories
by Sir Arthur Quiller-Couch

Bugler & Officer of the Rifles
by William Green & Harry Smith

The Compleat Rifleman Harris
by Benjamin Harris
to be released April 2006

Surtees of the Rifles
by William Surtees
to be published April 2006

Hussar in Winter
by Alexander Gordon
to be released May 2006

An extract from
Rifleman Costello
by *Edward Costello*
Published by Leonaur

All things arranged, we passed the gates of Brussels, and descended the wood of Soignies, that leads to the little village of Waterloo. It was the 16th -- a beautiful summer morning -- the sun slowly rising above the horizon and peeping through the trees, while our men were as merry as crickets, laughing and joking with each other, and at times pondered in their minds what all this fuss, as they called it, could be about; for even the old soldiers could not believe the enemy were so near.

We halted at the verge of the wood, on the left of the road, behind the village of Waterloo, where we remained for some hours; the recruits lay down to sleep, while the old soldiers commenced cooking. I could not help noticing while we remained here, the birds in full chorus, straining their little throats as if to arouse the spirits of the men to fresh vigour for the bloody conflict they were about to engage in. Alas! How many of our brave companions, ere that sun set, were no more! About nine o'clock, the Duke of Wellington with his staff, came riding from Brussels and passed us to the front; shortly afterwards, orders were given to the Rifles to fall in and form the advanced-guard of our division, and follow. We moved on through the village of Waterloo, and had not proceeded far, when, for the first time, we heard distant cannon; it was, I believe, the Prussians engaged on our extreme left.

About three o'clock in the afternoon we arrived at four roads; at this time there was a smart firing going on in our front; this, I believe, was caused by some Belgians playing at long shot with the enemy. Here I again saw the Duke of Wellington looking through his glass, as we halted a few moments; this was at Quatre Bras, and immediate orders were given by one of the Duke's staff to occupy a clump of trees a little on our left; our company were ordered to take possession of it.

While performing this task I could see the enemy emerging from a wood about a mile on our right, which was rather on a hill, with a clear plain between us. We had scarcely taken possession of the wood, when, for the first time, I beheld a French cuirassier on vidette. He was in an instant fired at by our men and his horse shot under him; he disengaged himself from the stirrups as the horse was falling, waving his sword over his head to put us at defiance, but he was immediately dropped by another rifle shot. I think I can venture to assert that our company was the first of the British army who pulled a trigger at this celebrated battle.

The enemy's light troops, I could soon perceive, in extended order, and in great force coming down to oppose us. This caused a corresponding movement on our part, and we were ordered to take ground to our left, passing close to a pond of water, the main road separating us from the enemy. While executing this, the French commenced a very brisk fire on us, until we gained possession of a few houses on the main road on a rising ground, which two companies of our Rifles instantly occupied. The remainder of our division was now enveloped in one blaze of fire on the plain before mentioned. But we remained very quietly where we were, until the French bringing up some artillery, began riddling the house with round shot. Feeling rather thirsty, I had asked a young woman in the place for a little water, which she was handing to me, when a ball passed through the building, knocking the dust about our ears; strange to say, the girl appeared less alarmed than myself.

Fearing that we might be surrounded, we were at length

obliged to leave the building, in doing which we were fiercely attacked by a number of the French voltigeurs, who forced us to extend along a lane, from whence we as smartly retaliated, and a galling fire was kept up for some time on both sides.

It is remarkable that recruits in action are generally more unfortunate than the old soldiers. We had many fine fellows, who joined us on the eve of our leaving England, who were killed here. The reason of this is, that an old rifleman will seek shelter, if there be any near his post, while the inexperienced recruit appears as if petrified to the spot by the whizzing balls, and unnecessarily exposes himself to the enemy's fire.

An extract from
Captain of the 95th (Rifles)
by Jonathan Leach
Published by Leonaur

Lord Wellington now ordered the infantry to retire in columns, covered by the cavalry and horse artillery. No man who was present can possibly have forgotten that magnificent sight, nor the steadiness and extreme regularity with which the columns fell back over this extensive plain, followed and assailed in flanks and rear by overwhelming numbers of cavalry and artillery.

During this retreat we were exposed to a constant cannonade, and threatened by heavy masses of infantry, ready to close with us if our pace was relaxed for a minute. Nor was the steadiness and gallantry displayed by the cavalry and horse-artillery less worthy of admiration. A halt of two or three minutes would have enabled the French infantry to reach us. Thus we marched some miles over a country as level as a chessboard, in columns of battalions, ready to engage the French infantry if they should overtake us, and equally so to receive their cavalry, in square or close column, if they attempted to charge. The beautiful series of evolutions of the two armies on this day, and on the three following, were such as a man may never witness again if he lives for ages.

The heat was suffocating, and there being no water on this sun-burnt plain, numbers of men dropped on the road, and, of course, fell into the hands of the enemy, as we could not stop to bring them along. Many soldiers, particularly of the Portuguese, died on the road, from the heat and want of water. At length we arrived at the edge of this elevated plain, which looks down on the Guarena, a small river in the hot months; and when we reached it, man and horse made a rush to quench their thirst. I have never quite forgiven our pursuers for pounding us with round shot from the heights above, and not allowing us time to swallow a mouthful of the lukewarm, muddy beverage, without the accompaniment of a nine-pound shot.

Soon after we had got into a position, on some high ground not far from the river, a column of infantry endeavoured to turn our left. The 27th and 40th regiments were posted there, and, by a volley, a cheer, and a resistless charge with the bayonet, instantly drove back the French, taking a general officer and upwards of two hundred men prisoners, killing and wounding many more. During the remainder of the day we were tolerably quiet. A hot wind with a thick suffocating atmosphere set in and lasted a day or two.

It is worthy of remark, that the horse artillery which accompanied our advanced and rear-guards, consisted of light six-pounders only, whereas the artillery attached to the French advanced and rear-guards were usually eight-pounders, equal to British nines. It is obvious, therefore, that our people always laboured under a great disadvantage in this respect, as the French could batter and pound us at such a distance as it was not in the power of our light six-pounders to return with effect. I have heard officers of our artillery complain of this, and have frequently witnessed the fact myself. Surely, if the cats of horses in the French army could drag along, at a pace sufficient to keep up with their cavalry, nine-pounders, the beautiful and powerful English horses belonging to our horse artillery were equally capable of drawing guns of the same weight of metal, and at a much more rapid rate, if required.

It is to be hoped that those who have the direction of affairs at Woolwich, have already considered those matters, and that they will adopt measures accordingly. It is equally desirable that those at the head of the British cavalry should bear in mind, that the French dragoons and chasseurs à cheval were armed during the Peninsular war with a long fusée, which could throw a ball as far as the musket of an infantry soldier, and that our dragoons, on the contrary, both light and heavy, were armed with a little pop-gun of a carbine. The consequence of this was, that when bodies of cavalry met at a distance from their infantry, the French dragoons often dismounted where the country was intersected and woody, and shot at our dragoons at a distance which rendered our short carbines almost useless. I appeal to old Peninsula cavalry men and officers for the accuracy of my statement.

An extract from
Napoleonic War Stories
by Sir Arthur Quiller-Couch
Published by Leonaur

Early next morning Sergeant Wilkes picked his way across the ruins of the great breach and into the town, keeping well to windward of the fatigue parties already kindling fires and collecting the dead bodies that remained unburied.

Within and along the sea-wall San Sebastian was a heap of burnt-out ruins. Amid the stones and rubble encumbering the streets, lay broken muskets, wrenched doors, shattered sticks of furniture -- mirrors, hangings, women's apparel, children's clothes -- loot dropped by the pillagers as valueless, wreckage of the flood. He passed a very few inhabitants, and these said nothing to him; indeed, did not appear to see him, but sat by the ruins of their houses with faces set in a stupid horror. Even the crash of a falling house near by would scarcely persuade them to stir, and hundreds during the last three days had been overwhelmed thus and buried.

The sergeant had grown callous to these sights. He walked on, heeding scarcely more than he was heeded, came to the great square, and climbed a street leading northwards, a little to the left of the great convent. The street was a narrow one, for half its length lined on both sides with fire-gutted houses; but the upper half, though deserted, appeared to be almost intact. At the very head, and close under the citadel walls, it took a sharp twist to the right, and another twist, almost equally sharp, to the left before it ended in a broader thoroughfare, crossing it at right angles and running parallel with the ramparts.

At the second twist the sergeant came to a halt; for at his

feet, stretched across the causeway, lay a dead body.

He drew back with a start, and looked about him. Corporal Sam had been missing since nine o'clock last night, and he felt sure that Corporal Sam must be here or hereabouts. But no living soul was in sight.

The body at his feet was that of a rifleman; one of the volunteers whose presence had been so unwelcome to General Leith and the whole Fifth Division. The dead fist clutched its rifle; and the sergeant stooping to disengage this, felt that the body was warm.

"Come back, you silly fool!"

He turned quickly. Another rifleman had thrust his head out of a doorway close by. The sergeant, snatching up the weapon, sprang and joined him in the passage where he sheltered.

"I -- I was looking for a friend hereabouts."

"Fat lot of friend you'll find at the head of this street!" snarled the rifleman, and jerked his thumb towards the corpse. "That makes the third already this morning. These Johnnies ain't no sense of honour left -- firing on outposts as you may call it."

"Where are they firing from?"

"No 'they' about it. You saw that cottage -- or didn't you? -- right above there, under the wall; the place with one window in it? There's a devil behind it somewheres; he fires from the back of the room, and what's more, he never misses his man. You have Nick's own luck -- the pretty target you made, too; that is unless, like some that call themselves Englishmen and ought to know better, he's a special spite on the Rifles."

The sergeant paid no heed to the sneer. He was beginning to think.

"How long has this been going on?" he asked.

"Only since daylight. There was a child up yonder, last night; but it stands to reason a child can't be doing this. He never misses, I tell you. Oh, you had luck, just now!"

"I wonder," said Sergeant Wilkes, musing. "I'll try it again, anyway." And while the rifleman gasped he stepped out boldly into the road.

He knew that his guess might, likely enough, be wrong: that, even were it right, the next two seconds might see him a dead man. Yet he was bound to satisfy himself. With his eyes on the sinister window -- it stood half open and faced straight down the narrow street -- he knelt by the corpse, found its ammunition pouch, unbuckled the strap and drew out a handful of cartridges. Then he straightened himself steadily -- but his heart was beating hard -- and as steadily walked back and rejoined the rifleman in the passage.

"You have a nerve," said the rifleman, his voice shaking a little. "Looks like he don't fire on redcoats; but you have a nerve all the same."

"Or else he may be gone," suggested the sergeant, and on the instant corrected himself; "but I warn you not to reckon upon that. Is there a window facing on him anywhere, round the bend of the street?"

"I dunno."

The rifleman peered forth, turning his head sideways for a cautious reconnoitre. "Maybe he has gone, after all -- "

It was but his head he exposed beyond the angle of the doorway; and yet, on the instant a report cracked out sharply, and he pitched forward into the causeway. His own rifle clattered on the stones beside him, and where he fell he lay, like a stone.

Sergeant Wilkes turned with a set jaw and mounted the stairs of the deserted house behind him. They led him up to the roof, and there he dropped on his belly and crawled. Across three roofs he crawled, and lay down behind a balustrade overlooking the transverse roadway. Between the pillars of the balustrade he looked right across the roadway and into the half-open window of the cottage. The room within was dark save for the glimmer of a mirror on the back wall.

"Kill him I must," growled the sergeant through his teeth, "though I wait the day for it."

And he waited there, crouching for an hour - for two hours.

He was shifting his cramped attitude a little -- a very little -- for about the twentieth time, when a smur of colour showed on the mirror, and the next instant passed into a dark shadow. It may be that the marksman within the cottage had spied yet another rifleman in the street. But the sergeant had noted the reflection in the glass, that it was red. Two shots rang out together. But the sergeant, after peering through the parapet, stood upright, walked back across the roofs, and regained the stairway.

An extract from
Bugler & Officer of the Rifles
by William Green & Harry Smith
Published by Leonaur

Bugler William Green:
The forlorn hope was composed of 350 men of the 43rd, 52nd, and Rifle Brigade, all volunteers, and two buglers from each regiment. Our bugle major made us cast lots which two of us should go on this momentous errand; the lot fell on me and another young lad. But one of our buglers who had been on the forlorn hope at Ciudad Rodrigo offered the bugle major two dollars to let him go in my stead. On my being apprised of it, he came to me, and said:

"West will go on the forlorn hope instead of you,"

I said "I shall go where my duty calls me." He threatened to confine me to the guard tent. I went to the adjutant, and reported him; the adjutant sent for him, and said:

"So you are in the habit of taking bribes;" and told him "He would take the stripes off his arm if he did the like again!" He then asked me "If I wished to go?"

I said "Yes, sir."

He said "Very good," and dismissed me.

Those who composed this forlorn hope were free from duty that day, so I went to the river, and had a good bathe; I thought I would have a clean skin whether killed or wounded, for all who go on this errand expect one or the other.

At nine o'clock at night, April 6th, we were paraded; it was then dark, and half-a-pound of bread and a gill of rum were served out to each man on parade. The party was commanded by Colonel M'Cloud of the 43rd regiment, Major O'Hare of the rifles, and Captain Jones of the 52nd regiment. We were told to go as still as possible, and every word of command was given in a whisper. I had been engaged in the field about 26 times, and had never got a wound; we had about a mile to go to the place of attack, so off we went with palpitating hearts. I never feared nor saw danger till this night.

As I walked at the head of the column, the thought struck me very forcibly "You will be in hell before daylight!" Such a feeling of horror I never experienced before! On our way to the wide ditch that surrounded the wall of the town, were laid small bags filled with grass, for each man to take up as he passed along to throw into the ditch to jump on, that we might not hurt or break our legs as the ditch was eight or nine feet deep; a party were in the rear with short ladders to be put into the ditch, and to be carried across for the men to ascend to the surface near the wall.

We had to pass between our batteries and the town; the artillery were firing blank cartridges, while we passed the guns; this we were apprised of, as being designed to keep the enemy from suspecting that we were to storm that night. There was no firing from the enemy until we arrived at the ditch. All had been still so far, but as the bags were thrown and the men descended, the enemy threw up blue lights; we could see their heads, and they poured a volley down upon us.

I was in the act of throwing my bag, when a ball went through the thick part of my thigh, and having my bugle in my left hand, it entered my left wrist and I dropped, so I did not get into the ditch. I scarcely felt the ball go through my thigh, but when it entered my wrist, it was more like a 6-pounder than a musket-ball! It smashed the bone and cut the guides, and the blood was pouring from both wounds, I began to feel very faint.

Our men were in the ditch, while the enemy had shells loaded on the top of the wall about two yards apart. As they were fired they rolled into the ditch, and when they burst, 10 or 12 men were blown up in every direction! However, some of them arrived at the breach, but a great many both killed and wounded lay around me; the balls came very thick about us, and we were not able to move. At length the whole of the light division came past me; my comrade, a sergeant, seeing me (for there was plenty of light!) said:

"Bill, are you wounded?"

I said "Yes, and cannot get up!"

He said "Here is a little rum in my flask, drink it, but I cannot assist to carry you out of the reach of shot."

His name was Robert Fairfoot. Shortly afterwards a musket ball struck him, went through the peak of his cap, and lodged in his forehead; the ball was extracted, he recovered, and through good conduct and his valour as a soldier, he obtained a commission, and was afterwards made adjutant of the regiment.

Harry Smith:

The key of the enemy's position was in our hands, and the great line was our next immediate object. We were speedily reformed, and ready for our attack on the enemy's line-position and strong field fortifications. In descending La Petite Rhune, we were much exposed to the enemy's fire, and when we got to the foot of the hill we were about to attack, we had to cross a road enfiladed very judiciously by the enemy, which caused some loss. We promptly stormed the enemy's works and as promptly carried them.

I never saw our men fight with such lively pluck; they were irresistible; and we saw the other Divisions equally successful, the enemy flying in every direction. Our Riflemen were pressing them in their own style, for the French themselves are terrific in pursuit, when poor dear gallant (Sir Andrew) Barnard was knocked off his horse by a musket-ball through his lungs. When Johnny Kincaid, his adjutant, got up to him, he was nearly choked by blood in his mouth. They washed it out for him, and he recovered so as to give particular orders about a pocket-book and some papers he wished sent to his brother. He did not want assistance; the soldiers loved him; he was borne off to the rear, and, when examined by Assistant-Surgeon Robson, it was found that the ball had not passed through, but was perceptible to the touch.

The surgeon had him held up, so that when he made a bold incision to let the ball out, its own weight would prevent its being repelled into the cavity of the chest. The ball was boldly and judiciously extracted, no fever came on, and in three weeks Barnard was at the head of a Brigade, with one wound still open, and in the passage of the Gave d'Oleron he plunged into the water, and saved the life of a soldier floating down the river.

But to the fight. Everything was carried apparently, and our Division was halted. Some sharp skirmishing was going on, and Colborne and I were standing with the 52nd Regiment, again ready for anything, on a neck of land which conducted to a stronglooking star redoubt, the only work the enemy still held, when Charlie Beckwith, the A.Q.M.G. of our Division, came up with orders from General Alten to move on.

"What, Charlie, to attack that redoubt? Why, if we leave it to our right or left, it must fall, as a matter of course; our whole army will be beyond it in twenty minutes."

"I don't know; your orders are to move on."

"Am I to attack the redoubt?" says Colborne.

"Your orders are to move on," and off he galloped.

Colborne turns to me, and says, "What an evasive order!"

"Oh, sir," says I, "let us take the last of their works; it will be the operation of a few minutes," and on we went in a column of companies.

As we neared the enemy, Colborne's brilliant eye saw they were going to hold it, for it was a closed work, and he says, "Smith, they do not mean to go until fairly driven out; come, let us get off our horses."

I was just mounted on a beautiful thoroughbred mare,

my "Old Chap" horse being somewhat done, and I really believed anything like fighting was all over. I said nothing, but sat still, and on we went with a hurrah which we meant should succeed, but which the garrison intended should do no such thing. My horse was struck within twenty yards of the ditch, and I turned her round so that I might jump off, placing her between me and the fire, which was very hot. As I was jumping off, another shot struck her, and she fell upon me with a crash, which I thought had squeezed me as flat as a thread-paper, her blood, like a fountain, pouring into my face.

The 52nd were not beat back, but swerved from the redoubt into a ravine, for they could not carry it. While lying under my horse, I saw one of the enemy jump on the parapet of the works in an undaunted manner and in defiance of our attack, when suddenly he started straight up into the air, really a considerable height, and fell headlong into the ditch. A ball had struck him in the forehead, I suppose -- the fire of our skirmishers was very heavy on the redoubt. Our whole army was actually passing to the rear of the redoubt. Colborne, in the most gallant manner, jumped on his horse, rode up to the ditch under the fire of the enemy, which, however, slackened as he loudly summoned the garrison to surrender.

The French officer, equally plucky, said, "Retire, sir, or I will shoot you!" Colborne deliberately addressed the men.

"If a shot is fired, now that you are surrounded by our army, we will put every man to the sword."

By this time I succeeded in getting some soldiers, by calling to them, to drag me from under my horse, when they exclaimed, "Well, d— my eyes if our old Brigade-Major is killed, after all."

"Come, pull away," I said; "I am not even wounded, only squeezed."

"Why, you are as bloody as a butcher."

I ran to Colborne just as he had finished his speech.

He took a little bit of paper out, wrote on it, "I surrender unconditionally," and gave it to me to give the French officer, who laughed at the state of blood I was in. He signed it, and Colborne sent me to the Duke.

When I rode up (on a horse just lent me), his Grace says, "Who are you?"

"The Brigade-Major, 2nd Rifle Brigade."

"Hullo, Smith, are you badly wounded?"

"Not at all, sir; it is my horse's blood."

"Well." I gave him the paper. "Tell Colborne I approve."

An extract from
The Compleat Rifleman Harris
by Benjamin Harris
Published by Leonaur

I remember meeting with General Napier before the battle of Vimeiro. He was then, I think, a major; and the meeting made so great an impression on me, that I have never forgotten him. I was posted in a wood the night before the battle, in the front of our army, where two roads crossed each other. The night was gloomy, and I was the very out-sentry of the British army. As I stood on my post, peering into the thick wood around me, I was aware of footsteps approaching and challenged in a low voice. Receiving no answer, I brought my rifle to the port, and bade the strangers come forward. They were Major Napier (then of the 50th foot, I think), and an officer of the Rifles. The major advanced close up to me, and looked hard in my face.

"Be alert here, sentry," said he," for I expect the enemy upon us to-night, and I know not how soon."

I was a young soldier then, and the lonely situation I was in, together with the impressive manner in which Major Napier delivered his caution, made a great impression on me, and from that hour I have never forgotten him. Indeed, I kept careful watch all night, listening to the slightest breeze amongst the foliage, in expectation of the sudden approach of the French. They ventured not, however, to molest us. Henry Jessop, one of my companions in the Rifles, sank and died of fatigue on this night, and I recollect some of our men burying him in the wood at daybreak, close to my post.

During the battle, next day, I remarked the gallant style in which the 50th, Major Napier's regiment, came to the charge.

They dashed upon the enemy like a torrent breaking bounds, and the French, unable even to bear the sight of them, turned and fled. Methinks at this moment I can hear the cheer of the British soldiers in the charge, and the clatter of the Frenchmen's accoutrements, as they turned in an instant, and went off, hard as they could run for it. I remember, too, our feeling towards the enemy on that occasion was the north side of friendly; for they had been firing upon us Rifles very sharply, greatly outnumbering our skirmishers, and appearing inclined to drive us off the face of the earth.

Their lights and grenadiers I for the first time particularly remarked on that day. The grenadiers (the 70th, I think) our men seemed to know well. They were all fine-looking young men, wearing red shoulder-knots and tremendous-looking moustaches. As they came swarming upon us, they rained a perfect shower of balls, which we returned quite as sharply. Whenever one of them was knocked over, our men called out "There goes another of Boney's Invincibles." In the main body immediately in our rear were the second battalion 52nd, the 50th, the second battalion 43rd, and a German corps, whose number I do not remember, besides several other regiments.

The whole line seemed annoyed and angered at seeing the Rifles outnumbered by the Invincibles, and as we fell back, "firing and retiring," galling them handsomely as we did so, the men cried out (as it were with one voice) to charge. "D—n them!" they roared, "charge! charge!" General Fane, however, restrained their impetuosity. He desired them to stand fast, and keep their ground.

"Don't be too eager, men," he said, as coolly as if we were on a drill-parade in Old England; "I don't want you to advance just yet. Well done, 95th!" he called out, as he galloped up and down the line; "well done 43rd, 52nd, and well done all. I'll not forget, if I live, to report your conduct to-day. They shall hear of it in England, my lads!"

A man named Brotherwood, of the 95th, at this moment

rushed up to the general, and presented him with a green feather, which he had torn out of the cap of a French light-infantry soldier he had killed:

"God bless you, general!" he said; "wear this for the sake of the 95th."

I saw the general take the feather, and stick it in his cocked hat. The next minute he gave the word to charge, and down came the whole line, through a tremendous fire of cannon and musketry—and dreadful was the slaughter as they rushed onwards. As they came up with us, we sprang to our feet, gave one hearty cheer, and charged along with them, treading over our own dead and wounded, who lay in the front. The 50th were next us as we went, and I recollect, as I said, the firmness of that regiment in the charge. They appeared like a wall of iron. The enemy turned and fled, the cavalry dashing upon them as they went off.

An extract from
Surtees of the Rifles
by William Surtees
Published by Leonaur

I had been in company with Captain Percival, my commanding-officer before alluded to, from the time of my first coming down to the division before daylight; and now he and I, hearing the heart-piercing and afflicting groans which arose from the numbers of wounded still lying in the ditch, set to work to get as many of these poor fellows removed as was in our power. This we found a most arduous and difficult undertaking, as we could not do it without the aid of a considerable number of men; and it was a work of danger to attempt to force the now lawless soldiers to obey, and stop with us till this work of necessity and humanity was accomplished.

All thought of what they owed their wounded comrades, and of the probability that ere long a similar fate might be their own, was swallowed up in their abominable rage for drink and plunder; however, by perseverance, and by occasionally using his stick, my commandant at length compelled a few fellows to lend their assistance in removing what we could into the town, where it was intended that hospitals should be established. But this was a most heartrending duty, for, from the innumerable cries of,—"Oh! for God's sake, come and remove me!" it was difficult to select the most proper objects for such care. Those who appeared likely to die, of course it would have been but cruelty to put them to the pain of a removal; and many who, from the nature of their wounds, required great care and attention in carrying them, the half-drunken brutes whom we were forced to employ exceedingly tortured and injured; nay, in carrying one man out of the ditch they very frequently kicked or trode upon several others, whom to touch was like death to them, and which produced the most agonizing cries imaginable.

I remember at this time Colonel (the late Sir Niel) Campbell passed out at the breach, and, as he had formerly been a Captain in our regiment, many of the poor fellows who lay there knew him, and beseeched him in the most piteous manner to have them removed. He came to me, and urged upon me in the strongest manner to use every exertion to get the poor fellows away. This evinced he had a feeling heart; but he was not probably aware, that for that very purpose both my commanding-officer and myself had been labouring for hours; but it soon began to grow excessively hot, and what with the toil and the heat of the sun, and the very unpleasant effluvia which now arose from the numerous dead and wounded, we were both compelled, about mid-day, to desist from our distressing though gratifying labours.

It was now between twelve and one o'clock, and though we had had a great many removed, a much greater number lay groaning in the ditch; but our strength was exhausted, for he was lame and unable to move much, and I had been obliged to assist in carrying many myself, the drunken scoundrels whom we had pressed into the service seldom making more than one or two trips till they deserted us. But my lamented friend and messmate, poor Cary, was still to search for, and, after a considerable time, he was found beneath one of the ladders by which they had descended into the ditch. He was shot through the head, and I doubt not received his death-wound on the ladder, from which in all probability he fell. He was stripped completely naked, save a flannel waistcoat which he wore next his skin. I had him taken up and placed upon a shutter, (he still breathed a little, though quite insensible,) and carried him to the camp. A sergeant and some men, whom we had pressed to carry him, were so drunk that they let him fall from off their shoulders, and his body fell with great force to the ground. I shuddered, but poor Cary, I believe, was past all feeling, or the fall would have greatly injured him. We laid him in bed in his tent, but it was not long ere my kind, esteemed, and lamented friend breathed his last. Poor Croudace had also died immediately after reaching the hospital, whither he had been carried when he was shot.

Thus I lost two of my most particular and intimate acquaintances, from both of whom I had received many acts of kindness and friendship. They will long live in my memory. Cary was buried next day behind our tents, one of the officers (my other messmate) reading the funeral service.

I cannot help adverting to some of the scenes which I witnessed in the ditch, while employed there as above noticed. One of the first strange sights that attracted our notice, was soon after our arrival. An officer with yellow facings came out of the town with a frail fair one leaning on his arm, and carrying in her other hand a cage with a bird in it; and she tripped it over the bodies of the dead and dying with all the ease and indifference of a person, moving in a ball-room,— no more concern being evinced by either of them, than if nothing extraordinary had occurred. It was really lamentable to see such an utter absence of all right feeling.

Soon after this the men began to come out with their plunder. Some of them had dressed themselves in priests' or friars' garments—some appeared in female dresses, as nuns, &c.; and, in short, all the whimsical and fantastical figures imaginable almost were to be seen coming reeling out of the town, for by this time they were nearly all drunk. I penetrated no farther into the town that day than to a house a little beyond the breach, where I had deposited the wounded; but I saw enough in this short trip to disgust me with the doings in Badajos at this time. I learnt that no house, church, or convent, was held sacred by the infuriated and now ungovernable soldiery, but that priests or nuns, and common people, all shared alike, and that any who showed the least resistance were instantly sacrificed to their fury. They had a method of firing through the lock of any door that happened to be shut against them, which almost invariably had the effect of forcing it open; and such scenes were witnessed in the streets as baffle description.

An extract from
Hussar in Winter
by Alexander Gordon
Published by Leonaur

We had some skirmishing with the enemy's advanced guard in the early part of the day, but in the afternoon they pressed us so hard that the regiment was halted, and formed in column of divisions on a small eminence, masking the guns of the horse brigade which were brought up to support us. On observing our position, the enemy retired, and we were ordered to occupy Cubilos, a small village at no great distance, where we found a company of the Ninety-fifth. So many horses had been sent forward, having become unserviceable for want of shoes, that the regiment at this period could scarcely muster four hundred in the field, many of which were lame or quite worn out with fatigue, and the remainder unable to trot. Considering the jaded state of our horses, and the fact that almost the whole of the outpost duty ever since the commencement of the retreat had fallen upon the Fifteenth, it might reasonably have been expected that one of the other regiments should have been appointed to this service; but it seemed to be a settled system of our leaders to save the Tenth and Seventh as much as possible, out of compliment to the Prince of Wales and Lord Paget.

It was almost dark when we arrived at Cubilos, and whilst the quartermasters were making arrangements for getting the troops under cover, the regiment was drawn up in close column on an open space of ground in the centre of the place. We had not remained long in this position, when we were surprised by a quick and irregular discharge of small arms; the bullets rattled against the walls and lodged in the roofs of the houses behind which we were sheltered.

This unexpected attack created a considerable degree of uneasiness, for the horses were so wedged together it was with difficulty they could break into file; and the communication betwixt the village and the highroad was through a narrow hollow-way, where, if a single horse had fallen, it would have occasioned a scene of confusion which must have led to the most disastrous consequences. Having been ordered for duty, I was engaged in telling off the picquet at a little distance from the column when the firing commenced; and strong patrols being immediately despatched to the assistance of the riflemen, who were skirmishing with our visitors, the intruders were soon put to flight. After the regiment was withdrawn from the village, it was determined by the commanding officer to bivouac; it is only extraordinary that under the circumstances he should for a moment have entertained the intention of passing the night in quarters. Three squadrons took up a position near Cubilos; the left squadron was detached half a mile to the rear, where a road struck off to Ponteferrado. Our advanced picquets and patrols were pushed close to the French outposts, and shots were exchanged occasionally when either party encroached too much on the other's ground. The weather was cold and frosty, but we collected fuel enough to supply several large fires; and, as the inhabitants had deserted their dwellings, we were forced to plunder the village in order to procure provisions and forage. But this was a necessary measure, and executed without any breach of discipline. Working parties were sent under the orderly officer and quartermasters to break open the houses, and abundant supplies of bread, meat, wine, corn, and hay, were found, which proved highly acceptable both to men and horses who had been but scantily provided with subsistence since we left San Christoval.

ALSO FROM LEONAUR
AVAILABLE IN SOFT OR HARD COVER WITH DUST JACKET

EW1 EYEWITNESS TO WAR SERIES
RIFLEMAN COSTELLO
by Edward Costello

The Adventures of a Soldier of the 95th (Rifles) in the Peninsula & Waterloo Campaigns of the Napoleonic Wars.

SOFT COVER : **ISBN 1-84677-000-9**
HARD COVER : **ISBN 1-84677-018-1**

RGW2 RECOLLECTIONS OF THE GREAT WAR 1914-18
WITH THE IMPERIAL CAMEL CORPS IN THE GREAT WAR
by Geoffrey Inchbald

The Story of a Serving Officer with the British 2nd Battalion Against the Senussi and During the Palestine Campaign.

SOFT COVER : **ISBN 1-84677-006-7**
HARD COVER : **ISBN 1-84677-012-2**

EW7 EYEWITNESS TO WAR SERIES
A NORFOLK SOLDIER IN THE FIRST SIKH WAR
by J. W. Baldwin

Experiences of a Private of H. M. 9th Regiment of Foot in the Battles for the Punjab, India 1845-6.

SOFT COVER : **ISBN 1-84677-023-8**
HARD COVER : **ISBN 1-84677-031-9**

EW8 EYEWITNESS TO WAR SERIES
A CAVALRY OFFICER IN THE SEPOY REVOLT
by A. R. D. Mackenzie

Experiences with the 3rd Bengal Light Cavalry, the Guides and Sikh Irregular Cavalry from the Outbreak of the Indian Mutiny to Delhi and Lucknow.

SOFT COVER : **ISBN 1-84677-024-6**
HARD COVER : **ISBN 1-84677-039-4**

AVAILABLE ONLINE AT
www.leonaur.com
AND OTHER GOOD BOOK STORES

ALSO FROM LEONAUR
AVAILABLE IN SOFT OR HARD COVER WITH DUST JACKET

EW15 EYEWITNESS TO WAR SERIES
THE COMPLEAT RIFLEMAN HARRIS
by Benjamin Harris

The Adventures of a Soldier of the 95th (Rifles) During the Peninsular Campaign of the Napoleonic Wars.

SOFTCOVER : **ISBN 1-84677-047-5**
HARDCOVER : **ISBN 1-84677-053-X**

EW14 EYEWITNESS TO WAR SERIES
ZULU 1879
Selected by D.C.F Moodic & the Leonaur Editors.

The Anglo-Zulu War of 1879 from Contemporary Sources; First Hand Accounts, Interviews, Dispatches, Official Documents & Newspaper Reports.

SOFTCOVER : **ISBN 1-84677-044-0**
HARDCOVER : **ISBN 1-84677-051-3**

RCI REGIMENTS & CAMPAIGNS SERIES
THE EAST AFRICAN MOUNTED RIFLES
by C.J. Wilson

Experiences of the Campaign in the East African Bush During the First World War (Illustrated).

SOFTCOVER : **ISBN 1-84677-042-4**
HARDCOVER : **ISBN 1-84677-059-9**

EW12 EYEWITNESS TO WAR SERIES
THE ADVENTURES OF A LIGHT DRAGOON IN THE NAPOLEONIC WARS
by George Farmer & G.R. Gleig

A Cavalryman During the Peninsular & Waterloo Campaigns, in Captivity & at the Siege of Bhurtpore, India.

SOFTCOVER : **ISBN 1-84677-040-8**
HARDCOVER : **ISBN 1-84677-056-4**

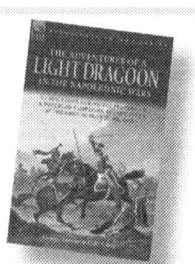

AVAILABLE ONLINE AT
www.leonaur.com
AND OTHER GOOD BOOK STORES